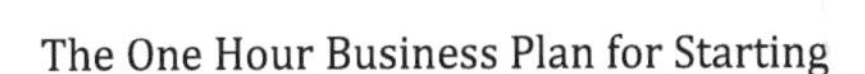

THE ONE-HOUR BUSINESS PLAN

FOR STARTING A SMALL BUSINESS:

ESCAPE THE 9 TO 5: THE SOLOPRENEUR'S GUIDE ON HOW TO WRITE A BUSINESS PLAN & START A BUSINESS.

BEGINNER TO ADVANCED SMALL BUSINESS PLANNER

Business Planning Series 1 ®

MARC ROCHE

Topics covered in this book: Business Plan, Business Writing, business plan book, business plan template, starting a small business, business planner and how to write a business plan.

Contributors & Influencers

This book was finished thanks to the contribution of **Jamie Forrest** for the Facebook marketing chapter. A special thank to him for the awesome advice.

I could not possibly list all the people who have influenced me through their work, but I will try to mention a few of the ones who spring to mind in no particular order. These are my business heroes, and without their contribution through their work, I would never have been able to write this book.

If you have never read their books, and are interested in business and entrepreneurship, I implore you to go out, and buy them and read them over, and over again.

Gary Vaynerchuk

Pat Flynn

Dan Meredith

Timothy Ferriss

Dale Carnegie

Danny Rubin

Hassan Osman

Megan Sharma

William Strunk Jr.

Sign up for exclusive resources + free e-books + tons of other resources and goodies at the end of the book

Never forget this...

"If you trust in yourself. . .and believe in your dreams. . .and follow your star. . . you'll still get beaten by people who spent their time working hard and learning things and weren't so lazy"

Terry Pratchett, The Wee Free Men

Contents

Get Marc Roche's Starter Library FOR FREE

Sign up for the no-spam newsletter and get an introductory book and lots more exclusive content, all for free.

Details can be found at the end of the book.

SECTION 1: INTRODUCTION TO BUSINESS PLANNING

1. Introduction to Business Plan Writing

If you are going to go into business for yourself, then you should be applauded. Being an entrepreneur is a very noble profession. You are helping the economy with your business, you might be employing people and you are in with a fighting chance of turning your own dreams into reality.

People say that if you find your passion then you will never work a day in your life. Unfortunately, having a passion is not going to cut it when you want your business to be successful. You can be as passionate as you want, but if you don't do the research and planning, then your business may be doomed before it even begins.

Think of it this way. If you were to go on a road trip across the U.S., you would have to have a general idea of where you want to end up (New York City) and where you want to start (Los Angeles), and you would need to know the various roads in the middle, or at least have a clear, accurate map.

If you were to just hit the road and go, well you might get to your destination, but it would take much longer, you may get lost and you might not enjoy the journey as much. Since you didn't plan where you would get gas, you may run out and end up stranded in the middle of nowhere. That is not going to make a great trip for you.

If you wanted to make the journey cheaper, smoother, faster and more comfortable, first, you would get a map and you would plan the journey down to the last detail. You would plan where to stay, where you to get gas and the best places to visit. It may be excessive, but now that you have planned everything you are going to have a quicker journey and there are going to be less hiccups. As long as you have a good, detailed plan and you follow through, adapting to any changes along the way, you will arrive at your destination.

This is essentially how this business plan is going to work for you. It is your road map to entrepreneurial success. It will detail what your business is, how it will compete, where the money is coming from and why customers will choose your business rather than your competitors'.

Without a business plan, even if you have a revolutionary product, the chances of success are greatly reduced. This business plan is your best friend when you are starting out with your company.

2. Why This Business Plan Book Works

A properly thought out business plan is a masterplan for future success, so it's really important that you create something that sells your ideas well.

Does your brain shut down to the idea when people tell you that you have to write a business plan if you want to be successful? Do you think to yourself, "that's for traditional or big businesses, not for businesses like mine"? or "you only need a business plan if you want funding from investors or banks, not for a simple idea like mine"?, or "I don't need a business plan, it's all in my head, business plans are for corporate types who like to justify their jobs with pointless paperwork and procedures". Well, you're wrong like Donkey Kong, trust me, I've made this mistake in the past. I've said all these things to myself and fallen flat on my face, before getting back up and making the same dumb mistake again.

You'd be surprised at how many people have a great idea but never do anything with it because "it's all too much". The sad part is that if they just put the work into writing a simple business plan, they'd know how to proceed.

The biggest mistake I made when I was just starting was to try to draw up a full corporate business plan for my first business. I spent hours going through this ridiculous corporate template and filling in the boxes with BS. I even copied and pasted things off the internet just to fill in some boxes. It just wasn't me, I was doing it because I had been told I should do it. The result was that I never looked at it again because it had nothing to do with me or my business. In subsequent businesses I simply refused to contemplate the idea of a business plan because it had been such a boring waste of time the first time around.

How did I not realize that the whole point of a business plan is that it needs to be individual and uniquely you? How did I not think, "what the hell am I doing"? Anyway, the moment I just simplified the whole process and tried to make it authentic and unique to my ideas, knowledge and objectives is the moment my whole perspective changed, and as a result my whole business changed.

If you know how to go about writing a business plan, it can actually be quite fun and rewarding as you see your ideas become more achievable before your very eyes. You also get an influx of new perspectives and ideas that you can use in your business.

There are many reasons to have a business plan in place when you are looking to start or grow your business.

Validate your Idea

First, it will test just how feasible the business is. If the business is not feasible, the business plan will show that, and you will be able to adjust your strategy or move on to a new idea that will be more successful.

Funding

If you want any sort of funding, from venture capitalists to your local bank loan, you are going to need a business plan. A business plan shows you have done your due diligence and is going to attract investors.

Goals and Strategy

A business plan is not just about starting a business, as the next section will show. A business plan will help you find ways to expand your successful business, to understand the roles of employees and to determine the future goals of the company.

WHAT NOW?

Your business plan is your pocket guide to where you are going and should be ever changing and adapting to market changes. Don't just write it and stick to it religiously, make sure you change it to suit new conditions, new information and new trends you encounter. Writing your business plan should be as creative as it is scientific. You can explore new ideas and tactics here. Test, evaluate, adapt and test again!

Now that we have gone over what kinds of business plans there are and why you need to write a business plan, we are almost ready to start writing. Before that is done though, it is all about asking the right questions for your business plan. Going back to the US trip scenario, before you go anywhere you are going to be asking yourself why you are traveling to that destination, how you are planning to get there, where you will go when you are there and when you want to go there. The same is true for your road map to business success.

Let's dive into the questions to ask yourself before you write your business plan.

Your business plan will help you see how likely you are to succeed and if your idea is financially viable. You'll also set logical goals and finish your concept. You'll probably get several new ideas you hadn't thought about while you're crafting your plan. This is good, just make a note and see if there's a sensible way of incorporating them.

The effort you invest into your plan will help you identify and avoid possible mistakes which could cost you a lot of time and money, thereby increasing your chances of being successful.

Just a final note to finish off this section, it's always a good idea to clearly state your 'value proposition' and keep it central to your plan. You can even write it on the top corner of every page if the plan is just for you. You can think of it as your main reason for being. Your value proposition should answer the following questions; "what problems are you solving for customers or clients?", "how are you better than your competitors?" and "why will you succeed when other similar businesses have failed?"

3. Business Plan Writing Skills

A business plan is all about balance. Too short and you don't get the information across or you look like you rushed the plan. Too long and you bore the reader, so they lose interest in the business plan.

Cut the Crap and Stand out from your Competition.

In this section, you'll learn the principles of clear, powerful business writing.

Good business writing is going to be easy to read. You must remember that the person looking at the plan is not going to just sit there and read it. They are looking at e-mails, sitting in meetings, talking on the phone and more. They will skim it, rather than read it usually. Therefore, you don't want to get too bogged down with giant paragraphs and long-winded sentences.

A typical business plan is going to be no more than 40 pages usually. That may seem like a lot, but you may need to have lists and graphs and pictures in there too, depending on your audience. You should be able to get your thoughts on paper in about 20 to 30 pages at most. Add in 10 pages for the resumes of your staff, projections and more and you have about 30 to 40 pages. If you end up going over 40 pages, you are getting too long-winded.

CLARITY IS KING:

Formal, "corporate" style language is full pointless jargon and unnecessarily complex explanations of simple concepts.

You should keep your business plan as simple as possible, so avoid using too many empty adjectives and adverbs unless you need them.

Words like "exactly," "precisely" and "really," often don't add any value to the sentence.

Can you think of anything more mind-numbingly frustrating than struggling through a business plan, trying to make sense of the unnecessarily complicated and pretentious language which should be explaining crucial things you need to know? Don't waste people's valuable time, express your message clearly and concisely.

Clarity shows confidence and respect for your readers. If you're writing a business plan and pitching it to investors, you're probably dealing with smart people just like yourself. Smart people see straight through jargon and unnecessarily complex language in a heart beat. It annoys them most of the time because it's insulting. It's insulting to assume they'd fall for such an obvious trick. Don't insult your readers, remember that less is more in most cases.

For example:

“improving the efficacy of measurable learning outcomes” could be "improving learning" or "improving learning efficiency" if you want to complicate it a bit.

4. When Should I Write a Business Plan?

Your business plan or business plans, should be continually adapted and tweaked to exploit the changes in the market and the business. A static business plan that gets forgotten at the bottom of your draw is useless.

The type of business plan you choose to write should depend on which stage of business you are at, but as a rule, you should start by exploring the different possibilities of your business first. You should then test some of those possibilities in the market and write an initial business plan based on that.

If you are expanding and you are doing a growth business plan, then you should focus on doing the business plan when your company is established and successful.

A business plan is not just about getting funding, it is about creating the road map for the success of your business. When you get down to writing your business plan, you should at least have your idea down on paper and an understanding of where you want to go. Once you have that, get down to writing your plan!

If you need funding, your business plan should come when you have made a detailed analysis of how much you believe you will make, how much it will cost to get off the ground and how much money you, or your friends and family, are providing.

If you have funding already, then a plan can be held off slightly until you get your business off the ground. At that point, the business plan is not about getting funding but creating a more detailed road map for yourself and your company.

5. Common Mistakes in Business Plans

Avoid the most common pitfalls so you can write an attractive business plan.

Before we get down to the nitty gritty of writing a business plan, it's useful to review possible fatal errors so you can avoid them. This is particularly important if you're looking for funding from investors or lenders.

STICK TO THE FACTS:

The first thing you need to remember is that sticking to the facts is what's going to give you credibility. Nobody, including yourself, deserves to have to sit through a pie in the sky business plan. Sticking to the facts is everything, particularly when analysing your competitors. You need to be precise and say, in simple English, exactly what you're going to do. Trying to confuse the reader is a fool's game, so respect your reader.

So, while it's great to put your ambitions down on paper for yourself and for investors to see, your plan needs to focus on real tangible areas like finance, demographics, product(s), branding and distribution channels for example.

IDENTIFY YOUR COMPETITORS:

If you're interested in finding funding it's essential that you identify your competitors and show that you've done your due diligence in this area. Not doing this property will give the reader the impression that you've not done your job properly. If they think this, you will have lost their trust from the get go.

Eve if you're only writing this business plan for yourself it's incredibly important that you do things properly. Every business has competitors, even if those competitors are in other similar sectors and compete indirectly. Doing this part thoroughly can bring you new insights and clarify existing doubts or misconceptions.

HOW WILL YOU MAKE MONEY?

When I started my first few "businesses", it's a bit generous to call them that, I didn't realise it at the time, but I focused on what I wanted to start based on some superficial idea of what a 'real business' was like. I saw other businesses and thought to myself something along the lines of "that looks nice, it must be making money because it's got a nice office and a nice website". I then tried to replicate that concept in my own way. This was obviously not a good way to start a business, I know that now.

If you focus excessively on 'starting a business' to impress either yourself or your friends and family, your business plan is not likely to work. Remember that in any business profit is king.

If you have members of staff, whether they're real or remote, add a short profile of each member of the team. If you don't have anyone to add yet but you plan to take on help in the next few months, create an avatar of the person or people you need.

The reason for adding profiles and /or avatars, is first of all to make potential investors comfortable with your business.

If they're investing money into your business, then it will help if they can see who will be working on the project. The second reason is for you to be able to see clearly on paper who you'll be working with. When you put things on paper you see them in a more sober light. This might help you decide which skills you actually need and which you don't. It may also give you some perspective on that person you think is really cool and nice to work with but who actually brings very little to the table.

NUMBERS

Work your numbers out before you seek investment or loans:

Make sure you know your numbers inside out. This will give you confidence and also credibility in front of investors and lenders

The money you're asking for needs to go with your needs. For example, if you ask for a $50,000 investment or loan, the person or business providing the money is going to want to know what you need it for, whether it's for marketing, production costs, inventory or wages. You need to be able to account for every penny or they'll lose trust in you, and if this happens they won't invest.

Getting someone else to write your business plan is dangerous in my experience. Not only can it affect cohesiveness, but it will defeat one of the main purposes of the plan; knowing your business.

We've looked at common mistakes people make when they write a business plan, now we're going to look at strategies for writing a strong business plan.

6. How Can I Provide Value?

Before you write your business plan, ask yourself about the core values of your company and what purpose the company will serve.

How can you bring value to people?

Giving value should be at the core of your existence as a business.

Will you be aiming to reduce the wait times for day cares in your community? Will you provide a place for customers to enjoy locally-made pasta dishes? Is it an Internet café in a community where there are no options for those without computers?

Knowing the purpose of your business will ensure that you have a compass for the decisions you are going to make in the future. It also provides you with an excellent starting point for your business plan. Within this question of what the purpose of your business is are two other very important questions.

- WHY: Why does your company exist, why will people buy your product or service and why will you and/or your employees get out of bed in the morning to work and make your company successful?

- HOW: How will you and your employees, if you have any, represent your company to its customers, how will the values of the company translate to success in the community and how will your customers know what you stand for?

7. What 's your Mission Statement?

When you decide to write a business plan, you need to know what your mission statement is going to be. Your mission statement is incredibly important, and it comes down to summarizing in one sentence why your company is in business and why customers will buy from you.

This relates to the previous questions about the purpose of your company, but more than that, the mission statement is a concise way to translate your entire business plan into one or two sentences.

Your mission statement is your vision for the company and what you want to accomplish. Before you start that business plan, outline about five different strategies that will help you accomplish what you plan to achieve.

8. What if Sh*t Hits the Fan?

What if something happens?. How do you deal with it? You need to know answers to these questions before you get down to writing your business plan.

For example, what if you sell your product or service at a certain price point, what return will you get on that?

What if trends change and your product is no longer needed?

What if your product is more/less efficient or popular than originally planned, do you change your price point?

You need to look at scenarios for what can happen to your business before you write the business plan because that gives you a good idea of where your direction will be and how you will handle both successes and failures within the company.

9. Have you Tested it?

Whether it is a service or product, you need to at least test out your idea before you write your business plan. This is like creating a prototype before you start selling anything.

Maybe you want to open a coffee shop, but you test out the response to your coffee by providing it to friends and family and seeing what they think. You should talk to potential customers in your market and other entrepreneurs to see how viable the idea is. You should speak to industry experts and other experts to get their honest feedback.

This is about constructive criticism. You may want to open a coffee shop, but after talking to an expert or potential customer, your idea may evolve and you may come up with a better concept, which serves a particular niche. Talking with others and putting the idea out there will help you know the market, who will buy in that market and who competes in that market.

You can even test your product or service by creating social media and website profiles, combining them with social media ads, and testing and measuring the response against your target market. Gary Vaynerchuk is an advocate of this technique, as it saves you a lot of time and money, and it stops you from wasting your precious time creating products that no one will buy. If for some reason you haven't heard of Gary Vaynerchuk, I'd wholeheartedly recommend that you watched a few of his videos and consumed some of his content before you embark on writing your business plan.

As we will see ahead, testing things ahead of time before the business plan is written is key to your success. Before you ever write a business plan, research, research, research.

THE RESEARCH PHASE

This is the part where many people tend to cut corners or get lazy. When you want to create a company that sells a product or a service, you always need to research. This applies directly to the last question you are supposed to ask yourself, "have I tested it?"

You need to research everything about your business idea because that's the only way you will ever know if it is going to be successful or not.

FEASIBILITY STUDY:

The feasibility study analyses the main elements of your plan: your idea, the advantage you have over your competition, an avatar of your ideal customer and your daily activities. You should also have realistic numbers to predict your cash flows.

By writing up and then reading through your feasibility plan you'll quickly see if your initial idea is sound enough to go forward with or not.

After you've done your feasibility plan and are satisfied that everything makes sense, it's always a good idea to discuss your business with impartial experts you trust to get some feedback. If you have a business mentor, talk to him or her and get feedback. This part will help you identify and eliminate mistakes and any dangerous assumptions you're making.

LOCATION OF YOUR TARGET CUSTOMERS

The area you want to sell to is the first thing to research. What are the demographics? Are you selling video games in a retirement community? Probably not the best idea. You should ensure that you know your area, who lives there and what their habits are.

COMPETITION

The competition that you will be facing is very important unless you offer something truly unique. You have to be honest with yourself here. Unique isn't just unique because you say so. It has to be a truly different and memorable product or experience.

Going back to the coffee shop scenario, if there are 10 coffee shops in a 20-block radius, then a coffee shop might not be your best option for a business. This is where research comes in and why it is so important. It isn't just about how many businesses like yours there are in your area. It is also about researching their products and services. Maybe there are a bunch of coffee shops, but none offer free-trade coffee. If that is the case, then you have a niche you can fill, especially in a neighbourhood where something like that is important to the consumer.

These are just a few of the things that you need to research before you start on your business plan. The most important thing to remember when you do your research is your goal is to be an expert in your area, your product and your business, serve your customers and make profit. If you don't do your research, you won't know the potholes and pitfalls you can fall into down the road.

Knowing your Business and your Sector

You want to be able to quote facts and figures in your head in case someone asks you about your business. You need to know everything because if you are an expert in your business and its sector, you will do a much better job of selling it to others. If you're looking for investment and you don't do your research and then go into a meeting with investors without a business plan, that lack of research is going to show.

SECTION 2: WRITING YOUR BUSINESS PLAN

10. The Executive Summary

Now we are getting down to the nitty-gritty of all of this. You have looked at the types of business plans, you have asked yourself questions and you understand why a business plan is needed. Now you can begin writing the business plan. This is the hardest part because you need to take everything you learned in asking those previous questions and translate it into something that will woo investors, gain customers and help your business become a roaring success.

Let's begin.

EXECUTIVE SUMMARY

The opening section of your business plan is one of the most important parts because it can win or lose your reader.

People are busy and their time is very valuable, so you need to respect that. Your reader will get a impression of you and your business from the opening section and if the first impression is negative it's very difficult to reverse.

This is a snapshot of your whole business and it needs to fit perfectly with the rest of the plan.

Paragraph 1 should say the problem you will solve for your customers or clients and why you're different from your competitors.

Paragraph 2 should say who your target customers are, who your competitors are and how much you expect to make.

Then you need to write a short part about your staff or team. Who will you need to work with? Give some details about skills and experience.

The final paragraph needs to focus on finances, with projected income for at least the first year, but preferably the first 2-3 years. You should also detail how much money you need to start up the business. How much will you contribute? How much will lenders or investors contribute? The maximum length for the executive summary should be 2 pages (at the very most), so remember to keep it concise and clear. It's also probably best to write this section last, as you'll have a better idea of what to say and how to say it once you've written the other sections.

This is the first part of your business plan and it is where you sell your business initially. When you look at the back of a book, you get a brief idea of what the book is about. The executive summary functions in the same way by giving an overview of your business.

It will summarize your business plan, so that someone looking at it will get a quick idea of what you are selling, what you need from them and how you are going to succeed.

The executive summary must be very clear and concise. Don't get bogged down in information that is going to bore the reader. Get to the point and impress the reader from the start.

Therefore, you should think of the executive summary as the most important part of the entire business plan. It is the cover to the book, it is the trailer to the film, it is what sells the business plan before you sell the idea to the reader. If you don't get the attention of the reader with the executive summary, the reader is not going to keep reading. The business plan ends up in the trash and you end up scratching your head, not quite sure what went wrong.

The executive summary isn't just about selling the business idea to an investor. It is about selling it to your own employees and yourself. If you can't sell your business to yourself or your employees (if you have any) through the executive summary, you will never sell it to someone you want money from.

WHAT GOES IN AN EXECUTIVE SUMMARY?

The executive summary isn't a one paragraph analysis of your company. It is a detailed look at your entire business plan, in a summarized form.

- The Opportunity: What is the need of your product or service in the community or area? What opportunity does this present?

- Advantage: How will your business take advantage of the opportunity that exists?

- The Market: Who is the market that will buy the product or service? Will you create a new market?

- Business Mode: What is your product or service, and what is going to make it something the target market will go after?

- Marketing Strategy: How are you going to market your product or service? Describe in a brief way.

- Competition: Who else is in the market and how are you going to get a market share or create a new market? Do you have a competitive advantage other businesses? Can you offer customers something that they cannot get from your competitors?

- Financial Analysis: This is just a quick summary of the financial plan. You should have brief projections for income and expenses for the next two to three years.

- Owners: Who owns the company, how are they qualified and why will they make the business successful? You can also outline your staff in this area and how they will help the company.

- Plan Implementation: How will you take your company from this moment to opening its doors and beyond.

Other things that you can include, depending on where your business is in its planning stages are:

- Mission Statement: What is the purpose of your business and what is its philosophy.

- Company Info: Give a brief history of the company here. This applies more for an established business looking to expand.

- Business Highlights: Like Company Info, this is for a business that has begun to establish itself. If you have had success in the market and are now going into business for yourself, you can include your own highlights here.

- Future Goals: Where do you see the company going? What goals do you have for the company?

TIPS FOR WRITING THE EXECUTIVE SUMMARY

You should make sure you focus on just giving a summary, since that is literally what this section is called. Don't go into super-detail with everything. Don't waste the time of the reader. Keep it a summary because you go into greater detail later.

You need to make sure you keep positive language in your summary. That may seem self-explanatory, but it is a common pitfall to not always talk positive. Instead of saying "With funding, the company should be able to find success." Seems okay right? It'not. It is not positive, and it tells the reader the company and its staff are not sure of themselves. Instead, you should say "The company will be in an excellent position to dominate the market share and will find even more success with the proper funding."

The executive summary should not be more than two to three pages long at most. It is a summary don't forget, so don't pad things out. Get to the point and move on.

Appearance and Presentation

This is the first thing any reader will see when it comes to your business plan. If there are spelling errors, incorrect facts or figures, or anything that doesn't make it look polished, then the reader will notice. Read it out loud, polish it and make it concise, and read it again. Don't move on from the executive summary until you are sure everything looks perfect.

11. Company Description

The next part of your business plan should be the company description. This is where you explain who you are, what your company does and how it operates. You should also explain what the goals of the company are here. You are essentially introducing yourself in this section, and it tells the reader why your company is the right company to sell the product or service.

WHAT GOES INTO THE COMPANY DESCRIPTION?

The name of this section is straight-forward. You are describing your company, but there are some things you should include here beyond your company name.

- Company Name: Speaking of the company name, well you include that here. This must be the official name of your business as it is registered.

- Type of Business: Is your business an LLC or a corporation? Is it a partnership or a sole proprietorship/sole trader or equivalent? This is important information for the reader if you are seeking investment or joint ventures.

- Owners: Who are the people behind the company and what is their experience? How will they bring success to the company?

- Location: Where is your company located? Does it have multiple locations? Do you have a headquarters for the company?

- History: This may not be very long if you are a new small business, but you can still go into detail about the company and how the idea for it came about. What inspired you to create the business? Let your passion tell the history.

- Product/Service: So, what are you selling? Why are you selling it? Give a brief overview here of the product or service and who you want to sell it to.

- Objectives: This just details what your immediate future goals for the company are and how you are going to achieve them.

TIPS FOR WRITING THE COMPANY DESCRIPTION

The first paragraph in your company description part should capture all the information of the company. You are essentially pitching your company here, so keep it quick and concise, but show your passion for the business and why you believe in it so much.

You are going to have a lot of the information about your company, the staff and the product later in the business plan, so you should keep only the top information in this section. Give a general overview of the information, without going down into too much detail.

I've said it before and I'll say it again... show the passion you have for your company and let it translate to the business plan and this section.

You need to show your excitement in your own words and through the tone of your writing. You don't want to produce another boring business plan that investors, lenders and potential partners will have to wade through or even throw in the trash. Be yourself, be authentic, be original and be professional at the same time.

This section shouldn't be too long, maybe one to two pages. Don't let it go on too long. You should read through everything and cut out any information that doesn't need to be there. Keep it to the point and eliminate any duplicate or unnecessary information.

12. Product or Service

Now we're getting down to the nitty gritty. This is a very important section for your business plan because you have already sold your company to the reader, that's why they are still reading. Now you sell the product or service. It's here that you clearly describe what you're selling and why your customers or your clients are going to find value in what you're providing.

Just like everywhere else in your business plan, show your passion for the product or the service. If you aren't excited about the product, how do you expect the reader or a potential customer to be?

What Goes into the Product or Service Section?

This section is an in-depth look at your product or service. Within this section, you should have the following parts:

- **Description:** This is self-explanatory, but you need to describe your product here. Go into detail about it and explain how your product or service came about. Explain what it does, what it will do for the customer and why they will buy it. Don't hold back here, get right down to the nitty-gritty of the product here.

- Comparison: How does this product or service compare with other similar products or services? Compare it to those products and show not only how your product will set itself apart from them, but how the success of those products can translate into the success of your product or service.

- **Price Points:** Here you are going to list your price points and explain how you came to those prices, and how that will help you turn a profit. You will go into more detail on this later in the financial section.

- **Order Fulfilment**: For a product, you will explain here how you'll fulfil orders to your clients. You need to explain how you'll keep the item in stock, how many you can produce in a certain period and how you will meet any demand that may arise. How will you get the product or service to the customer? That is the main question you are answering here.

- **Special Items:** Does your product or service require special supplies or technology? Does it require certain software? It is here you explain the special items needed for your product or service and how you will ensure that the extra items don't make it harder for people to use your product, and therefore less likely to buy it.

- **The Future**: Lastly, you need to go into detail about the future of the product or service, how it will change and how it will adapt to a changing market. What will the new versions of it be and how will you get customers to buy those new versions if they already have the old versions. This section can sometimes be added later, as you adapt the business to changes in the market for example.

Production techniques:

Describe your production techniques and your schedule in detail. When you describe your production techniques take the opportunity to sell your company and your product again. Use attractive copy to immerse your readers in what you're all about.

You also need to mention your location and any equipment you use.

Final Tips for Writing the Product or Services Section

This section is about the product or service, but you should focus on the customer. You need to outline the benefits to the customer and why he or she will want it. You should explain the ideal customer and how your product or service is going to make their lives better. Essentially, who is your customer and why are they buying your product?

As with elsewhere, get right to the point. Don't dance around your product or service, just get down to explaining it. Get down to the need this product fills for the customer, or the problem you are solving for them.

Since this is a product you love, or a service you want to provide, you may be tempted to go on too long with your information. It is good to get a lot out there and explain a lot about what you are offering, but at the same time keep it simple. Don't get bogged down in industry jargon or anything like that. You need to assume that the person reading your business plan does not have an expert knowledge in your product or service, nor the industry it will be in, unless of course, the business plan is for your eyes only at the moment.

If you have a product or service that others have, like specialty coffee, then you need to explain in this section why you are unique. Embrace your uniqueness and show why you are setting yourself apart from the rest of the industry. Explain not only how your product or service is unique, but why it is better than the rest. Focus on benefits, not features.

Lastly, make sure you show your process, just like in Math class. What I mean by that is, show how you got to the information about your price point and why you calculated the price points as you did. Also, go into detail about how you are selling the product, and whether you are selling it online, in a retail location, on the road or anything else.

13. Market Analysis

An understanding of the industry you are getting into is vitally important if you want your business to succeed. For example, if you are interested in providing people with entertainment, that's good. What's not good is if it's 2009, you haven't been paying attention to the industry and you start up a video and DVD rental store. Chances are, it's going to fail. That is because the industry has changed, and people are not accessing media the way they used to.

Analyzing the market can also keep you on the cutting edge. When Netflix started, there was no real media streaming. High-speed internet was very new, and people still rented their content, bought it in physical form or downloaded it illegally. Netflix latched onto this idea, and while they provided physical copies at first, they looked at the market and saw that it was moving in the direction of streaming. When the time came, Netflix shifted quickly, and now the company is worth billions. Blockbuster on the other hand, was a household brand loved by millions of people worldwide, but they did not see the shift coming, or did not react in time due to poor leadership and now sadly they're gone.

The market analysis section is where you look at these types of trends and explain to those reading the business plan where you see the market going and how your product or service will succeed in it. It provides a detailed overview of the industry and you will have to have statistics within the section to back up everything you say.

The market analysis section will look at the industry, the market you are going to target, the competition in that market and where your product or service will be situated in the market. If you have a great deal of data to back up the claims you are making in this section, then that should be provided in the appendices at the end of the business plan.

What Goes into this Section?

In this section, you can divide the information up into the following parts.

- **Industry Description/Outlook**: This section will look at the industry you are starting your business in. It is where you will address the size of the industry, the growth of the industry, where the trends are and what the outlook of the industry happens to be.

- **Target Customer** (Ideal Customer): Who are you going to target with your product or service? Who is the customer that you want to reach? The information in this section must dive deep into the demographics of the customer group you are looking at reaching. This must include what the age range of your ideal customer is, their income level and what type of lifestyle they lead. In addition to this information, you should also look at the purchase potential of the individual customer, what their motivations are for buying your product and how you are going to reach that customer. It helps to give them a name, so that you can 'humanize' them as much as possible.

- **Market Test**: If you are going to release your product or service, you need to carry out some initial hard evidence about the market you're targeting. This is where you put the results of your investigation, including how you tested out the market and all the supporting statistics that you have. Be honest and impartial, don't lie to yourself here.

- **Lead Time**: This is a very important section because it will detail the amount of time it is going to take for any order to be completed. From the moment that your customer makes a purchase, how long will it take for them to get the finished product or service? How will you handle individual orders? How will you handle large volume purchases?

- **Analysis of Competition**: Who is going to be competing with you in the market? What are the strengths of the competition? What are their weaknesses? How will you outperform them? What are the problems standing in your way to keep you from competing against that competition?

TIPS FOR MARKET ANALYSIS

This is such an important section that it is vital that you get the information right, in a clear and concise manner. Here are some tips to help you do just that.

- The Internet is your best resource. It's where you'll get a lot of the information you're looking for. The Internet has demographic data, data on competitors, the market and much more. A lot of research has been done to gather the information you are looking for in order to have as much detail in the market analysis as possible. Google Keyword Planner is a great place to start. You can use this to visualise what people are searching for. Social media platforms can also be of great use. You can run a test advert for your product on Facebook for example, and then see the demographics of the people who have engaged with your ad.

- A great way to think about the market you are striving for is to think like the ideal customer. Look at the product or service through their eyes. What is the solution your product or service provides? Does the competition provide a better solution to the problem? How will your product help the customer in a better manner? Look at your product or service through their eyes and you will have a clearer idea of how you are going to succeed in the market.

- Before you dive down into the details of the market analysis, include a summary at the beginning of the section. This will help the person reading it know the most important parts of the summary right away and they can get a good first impression on your market analysis as a result.

- All the data that you compile for your market research should relate to the business you are launching. Make sure everything comes back to the business. Stay concise and don't go off on a tangent with the details. Keep things on a straight road. Like they say, cut to the chase.

- Lastly, have some great visual aids in this section, particularly if you will be showing it to other people. This is important because it will allow you to give the reader something to look at that breaks up the text. People tend to remember visual things better than the written word as well, so visual aids within this section will not only stand out more but stay in the mind of the reader more.

14. Marketing Strategy

You've shown what the market is like. You've analyzed it and presented your findings in a clear and concise manner. Now it's time to show how you're going to get into that market. In this strategy, as the name suggests, you will show your plan for entering the market and making a profit.

The marketing strategy part of your business plan builds on what the market analysis section already delved into. In this part of the business plan, you outline where your business will sit in the market, how you will price your product or service, as well as how you will sell it and promote it as well.

I LOVE IT
WHEN A PLAN
COMES TOGETHER

What Goes into a Marketing Strategy?

Your marketing strategy shows you, your vendors, investors and your employees how you plan to sell your product or service. It will also show future marketing ideas you have. There are several important parts to the market strategy section.

- **Product:** In this part of the market strategy section, you need to explain your product and why it's going to sell in the market. This includes explaining the brand name, any products or services that are related to it, as well as the functionality of it. In the product area, you need to explain the quality of the finished product, what the warranty will be for it and even the packaging it will be sold in. This should be a more scientific description of the product or service than what we looked at in previous sections.

- **Promotion:** In this part, you cover the various parts of how you are going to market your product or service. In this section, you will address what your marketing budget will be, the promotional strategy and any publicity you plan for it. This also includes the advertising, who your sales force is and why they are qualified, and how you are going to handle sales promotions.

- **Price:** The price you charge for your product or service is incredibly important. Charge too much and you won't sell anything. Charge too little and you won't bring enough money in to be sustainable. Some of the things to address in the price section are how you will bundle the product or service with other products and services your company sells. You also need to explain how flexible you are on the price, and what your pricing strategy is going to be. The retail price should be addressed, as well as how you came to that number. In addition to the retail price, you need to address the seasonal price of your product if it is applicable and any wholesale prices you may offer for larger volume orders.

- **Place:**

- How are you going to deliver your product or service to the customer?
- Will you have distribution centers or distribution channels?
- How will you handle inventory management, as well as the logistics of the orders if you're selling physical products?
- How will you process the orders?
- Do you need a transportation network?
- Will you be keeping the product in a warehouse?
- Will you distribute your product or service through the Internet, by truck or another distribution method?

TIPS FOR YOUR MARKET STRATEGY SECTION

If you are more about ideas and managing, determining a marketing strategy may seem like a daunting task. To make it easier, I've compiled some tips to help get your marketing strategy off the ground and ready to roll into your business plan.

The first thing you need to do is ensure that your marketing strategy is unique in some way.

Let's look at PayPal. When they first started out, they literally paid customers to be customers if they referred someone. After a few months, they paid less for referrals until they had finally ended the program after a few years, spending tens of millions of dollars. That allowed the company to expand its customer base heavily, and it's now a company worth billions. In order to make your strategy unique, you should have a unique selling proposition. This is how you will explain how your marketing differs from other companies in your industry.

Be flexible with your marketing strategy.

Try different things, let some things stick and others not. Don't be afraid to try out some promotional ideas in your business plan that are way out of the box, and some that are standard. Do your research and don't expect any one method to make you millions over-night, it's all a learning curve.

When you determine what your pricing is going to be, you should have the data to back up why you are pricing the product for that certain amount.

Include ads from your competition, reports from the industry and any research you have conducted yourself.

As with the previous section, the marketing strategy should use visuals quite a bit.

Include charts, graphs, and anything that gets the information and facts out in a way that will be easy for your reader to understand.

Do not forget about your budget when you are doing your marketing strategy section.

Keep in mind the numbers from your financial analysis and translate that into how you will budget the promotion of your company and make a profit based on the price. You absolutely need to tie it into your financial status.

15. Management Summary

Think of your business as a ship and the ship has a crew. You have the map towards your business success, but you need someone to help on that ship. This is where your management team come in. They are your crew and a good crew will make your business successful.

In the management summary section of your business plan, you outline who the management of your business is and how they are going to make your business successful. This section backs up everything you have said in the business plan by showing your team of experts and what resources you have behind you at the company. Now this doesn't mean that you have to go out an employ a bunch of managers, it just means that you need to plan which jobs would be best done by other people. They could do the job in person if your business requires it, or remotely, like virtual assistants, content managers etc.

WHAT IS IN THE MANAGEMENT SUMMARY SECTION

There are several important parts of this section, which get down deep into who your business employs.

- **Business Structure:** What type of business do you have? Is it a partnership? Is it just you? Have you registered as a corporation? This is all outlined in this part.

- **Management:** If you're a solopreneur, then this would be just you. However, if you've got other people involved then; who is the team that is looking over the company? If you have formed your company into a corporation, who will sit on the board of directors. In this part, you would probably want to include an organizational chart that outlines who manages what in the company.

- **Other Individuals**: Other than your board and your employees, what other support do you have externally in the company? This includes your accountants, any professionals who handle your public relations, administrative support and any attorneys. If you're a solopreneur, then you need to outline who is going to help you with the different parts of the business. Do you have a content manager, a virtual assistant, an accountant?

- **Growth Plan:** In this section, you will look at the salaries of the employees in the company over the next few years. This gives a clear indication on your current and future payroll costs.

TIPS FOR THE MANAGEMENT SUMMARY

Of all the sections in the business plan, the management summary is probably the easiest to write. It's a very important section though, due to the fact that it analyzes the potential of the company and the employees in it.

- **Explain Things**: In this part, you want to describe how the employees in the company interact with each other. Go into a bit more detail beyond what your organizational chart says. How do roles cross over? Who handles multiple aspects of the company's operations?

- **Relate Experience**: How does the experience of each employee relate to the role they play in the business? Does the person handling the accounting have a strong background in accounting? Is your IT person someone with a lot of experience? These things sound obvious, but if you don't plan them it's easy to assume things and then pay the price when you're wrong.

- **Keep It Simple**: Don't go into too much detail about the biographical information of the employees. If you want to put in full biographies of everyone, then you can do that in the appendix.

- **Everyone Is Involved**: If you have employees, partners or managers you want to make sure that everyone has a look at this section. Let them read what you have said about them. They may be able to add some extra details to what you have already said in the business plan. This also ensures what you say is accurate.

16. Financial Analysis

In this incredibly important section, you want to make sure that you outline all the data for the financing of your business. What will your business need to expand and grow? What are the estimated operating expenses of your business? These are all important questions you will be answering in this section.

If you don't have a background in finance, then it could be a good idea to hire a financial advisor to handle this, or an accountant. Having accurate data is incredibly important here, so you want to make sure that a qualified person is handling this section if possible, but you also need to understand the principles yourself, so that you have a handle on the reality of your business.

WHAT IS IN THE FINANCIAL ANALYSIS SECTION

Within this section, you are going to delve deep into the finances of your business. It could be very dry reading for some, but it is vitally important to ensuring that your business is successful and that you are giving the reader an accurate representation of not only where your company is now, but where it's going.

-**Balance Sheet:** You should have a rundown of your finances, including any equity the business has, any liabilities and all assets.

-**Cash Flow Analysis:** This looks at the cash coming into the company based on what you forecast the sales of your product or service will be. You then subtract the expenses of running the business. This provides you with a cash flow analysis.

-**Profit-Loss Analysis**: This is an income statement, which takes the costs of the business activities minus the earnings over a specified period.

-**Break-Even Analysis:** What is the cost of doing business? This is always a vital question and a break-even analysis looks at the point where the cost of doing business is covered by sales. How much does your company need to stay in business without losing money, but not gaining any money?

- **Personnel Expenses**: If it applies, what are the expenses of your team? How much does it cost to get them everything that they need?

Keep it Realistic

It's vital that the numbers you include in these statements are supported by solid proof. The proof can be from historical data, market research or any credible source as long as it's logical. Some people even draft a 'worst case scenario' version and a conservatively optimistic version to see both ends of the spectrum. If you do this just change your assumptions about the key numbers so that the calculations are as accurate as possible.

More Tips for this Section

Since this section can be a bit complicated, these tips can help make it easier for you to navigate the tricky financial section if you're not a numbers person.

- First things first, make good assumptions; it's all about making informed guesses. Don't be afraid to make some assumptions over where you see the company going in terms of its finances. The most important thing in this section when assuming the future is to keep things consistent and to allow yourself and other potential investors, to make informed decisions based on sound data.

- As was mentioned before, you might need some help with this section after you've done the initial statements. To lower the stress of figuring out financials, have a professional come in and help.

- Remember in this section to include where the data comes from, what the numbers mean and don't forget about the generally accepted accounting principles, which are a collection of rules that define accepted accounting practice.

- Make sure your math is accurate. One small mistake could result in you having all your financials out of whack.

- Lastly, include some visuals. Show graphs and visual representations of your data to help the reader better understand it. You can also put supporting graphics in your appendix.

KEY FINANCIAL PROJECTIONS:

There are four basic kinds of financial statement that your business plan should include:

1. Balance sheet

2. Profit-Loss Analysis (Income Statement)

3 Cash-flow statement

4. Break-even Analysis

17. Your Balance Sheet

The balance sheet shows the financial health of your business or project and it's one of the main financial statements of a business plan, together with the profit and loss analysis and the cash flow statement. The balance sheet reflects your business' assets, liabilities, and equity.

Starting Your Balance Sheet

The basic equation for your balance sheet is that your **assets equal your liabilities plus your equity or your (or stockholders' equity.**

Assets = Liabilities + Equity.

A well-kept balance sheet is a key part of any successful project. It may seem tedious to make and update, or you may feel intimidated by the idea of it all, but the consequences of not having one, or not maintaining one, can be enough to break your business.

I'm going to try to deconstruct what a balance sheet is, and how to make and maintain your own.

There are three essential components that need to be listed on a small business balance sheet: assets, liabilities, and owner's equity. Assets refer to what your business owns and how much that's worth. Conversely, liabilities are what your business owes and how much that is worth. Finally, owner's equity reflects the financial investments of yourself and any business partners you may have.

This may all seem simple enough, but it can be difficult to know exactly what to write down on a sheet and how to categorize it. Moving through the categories one-by-one, you'll learn exactly how to format your balance sheet.

Assets

Assets should always be listed first on your balance sheet.

Line 1 lists your business' cash account. Most businesses have cash on hand either to facilitate day-to-day transactions (any business with a storefront, for example) or they have cash on hand for emergency scenarios or situations where other forms of currency simply won't suffice.

Line 2 is for accounts receivable, which is money owed to you by customers and clients. Obviously, this number will always be in-flux as you receive money from these individuals, or they accrue even higher debts with your business. The number reflected on you report is only expected to be accurate for the day it was created and by no means do you need to keep it up-to-date on a daily basis.

Line 3 is for the inventory of your business. This line states the current value of the products you sell based on their market value and the quantity you possess.

The final line for assets is **Line 4**, which is reserved for fixed assets. Fixed assets are things your business owns and uses for operation including land, buildings, vehicles, and equipment. The nature of fixed assets is that they are generally big-ticket items; you don't need to list every pencil and sheet of paper your company owns. Keep in mind that fixed assets generally depreciate over time. After all, you can't expect a company vehicle to hold the same value after several years of use.

All of your assets will be totalled on **Line 5**, which represents the total value of everything your business owns.

Liabilities

This category is far less pleasurable to tally up than the previous one but it's still key.

Line 6 is accounts payable; the polar opposite of accounts receivable. This line represents short-term debts you have with any suppliers or manufacturers you work with. Much like accounts payable, these fluctuate frequently are only expected to be accurate as of the day you publish your balance sheet.

Line 7 shows the total amount of loans you've taken out. Unlike accounts payable, these are long-term debts, often from a bank that last for more than a year. Many businesses use loans to stay afloat or to accommodate expansion.

Equity

Equity is listed in the same category as liabilities as it is money invested into the business.

Line 8 shows how much money has been invested by the owner as well as any other investors with a stake in the company.

Line 9 totals both liabilities and equity. The combined number should match Line 5, your total assets. If the numbers are not balanced, then your balance sheet is not correct. A company cannot own more than it owes. Take another look through your files and see if you've missed something.

Here's an example balance sheet to help you visualize what yours should look like:

Assets	**Value**
1.Cash	$25,000
2.Accts Rec	$300,000
3.Inventory	$175,000
4.Fixed Assets	$500,000
5.Total Assets	*$1,000,000*
Liabilities and Equity	**Value**
6.Accts Payable	$ 120,000
7.LT Bank Loans	$280,000
8.Owner's Capital	$600,000
9.Total Liability + Equity	$1,000,000

18. How to do an Income Statement

Income statements are a key part of effective recordkeeping for a business. They show whether your company has been profitable or not over a set timeframe. You can set the timeframe of your income statement to be whatever you please, but the most common timeframes are a month, a financial quarter, or an entire year.

"Profit and loss statement" is another term for this type of record, which should give you a better idea of exactly what it is. We'll break the process down line by line, so you know exactly how to properly format your own income statement.

Line 1 is for your gross revenue. This means the total amount of money you've made in sales, including sales made on credit that have not been collected yet. If you sold 50,000 units of product at $50 a unit then your line 1 would read $2,500,000.

Line 2 is the cost of goods sold. This refers to any and all costs directly incurred by your product. Expenses of this nature include the cost of manufacturing, raw materials, and labour related to the product. This line is usually the highest cost for any business.

If the 50,000 units you sold in line 1 were bought during that same timeframe at a cost of $25 a unit then that cost would be reflected in this line with the total of $1,250,000.

Line 3 is for your gross profit. Gross profit is simple to calculate. All you have to do is subtract line 2 (cost of goods sold) from line 1 (gross revenue). In our example this would be $1,250,000 ($2,500,000 - $1,250,000).

Line 4 represents your office expenses. This category focuses on selling, general, and administration fees (S,G &A) and any expenses not directly related to the sale of your product. S,G&A factors in wages, commission, rent, legal fees, accounting fees and the like.

Utility costs such as electricity, heating, etc. can be included in this line or listed on a separate line as "utilities."

For our example, we'll list our expenses at $250,000

Line 5 is where your company's depreciation expense is listed. This line expresses the depreciating value of equipment and buildings owned by your company. This expense is primarily listed for tax purposes. Our example statement lists the total as $100,000.

Line 6 is for your operating profit. Operating profit is easily determined by subtracting lines 4 and 5 (office expenses and depreciation) from line 3 (gross profit). This number is more commonly known as the earnings before interest and taxes (EBIT). In our example this line would read $900,000.

Line 7 is for interest expenses. This tracks interest that has accrued on debts held by your firm. Calculating interest is a simple matter of multiplying the interest rate of your debt by the principal amount of that debt. In our example, the interest is shown to be $50,000.

Line 8 is for earnings before taxes and it is deduced by subtracting line 7 (interest expenses) from line 6 (EBIT).

Line 9 is the cumulative amount you pay in taxes. This covers federal, state, local, and payroll taxes. We're listing the total cost of taxes as $35,000.

Line 10 is where you list the earnings available to common shareholders. This is simply calculated by subtracting line 9 (tax expenses) from line 8 (earnings before taxes).

Line 11 is specifically for companies that hold investors and/or companies wherein the owner derives a salary from the profits. This line denotes the draw/dividend for these individuals

Line 12 represents your net income which is money that can be reinvested into the company. This number is found by adding all your expenses and then subtracting them from line

3 or more easily by subtracting line 11 (draw/dividend) from line 10 (earnings available to shareholders).

This is a basic example of an income statement. Your own income statement may be more complex and have a greater number of lines depending on what expenses you run.

Remember that your income statement is only as accurate as the data used to compile it, so be sure to be rigorous in recordkeeping.

Below is the example statement to help you visualize your own.

1. Gross Revenue	$2,500,000
2. Cost of Goods Sold	$1,250,000
3. Gross Profit	$1,250,000
4. Selling & Administrative Expense	$250,000
5. Depreciation	$100,000
6. Operating Profit (EBIT)	$900,000
7. Interest	$50,000
8. Earnings Before Taxes (EBT)	$850,000
9. Taxes	$30,000
10. Earnings Available to Common Shareholders	$820,000
11. Dividends/Owner Draw	$25,000
12. Net Income	$795,000

19. How to do a Cash-Flow Statement

Just like the income statement, the cash flow statement reflects your business' financial performance over a specific time-period. However, the income statement includes non-cash items like depreciation of equipment or other assets. It may not be as practical as the cash flow statement if you're a solopreneur who isn't looking for outside investment, but if you are seeking investment then it's essential. It is also useful for your accountant to do this anyway, as It can affect how much tax you have to pay at the end of the financial year.

Cash flow statements are integral to maintaining accurate finances. They're arguably more accurate than a profit and loss forecast, and they are especially helpful in determining whether or not your business can actually survive.

Essentially, a cash flow statement lists all of your incoming profits and outgoing expenses on a month-to-month basis. This means everything from loan payments to personal investments into the business to standard cash and credit transactions. You'll be recording expenses in the month they occur, rather than spreading them throughout the year. After all, if certain fees come due in September, then you'll need to know that you actually have the cash to pay them in September.

The advantage of this meticulous form of recordkeeping is that you'll know what months cost the most for your business to operate in, and what months promise the greatest profits. You can adjust your costs accordingly and if you find yourself coming up short in a month, you have time to take out a loan or seek alternative means of keeping things running.

Setting up a cash flow statement can be broken down into four simple steps.

1. Opening Balance

Your starting balance is exactly what it sounds like. The capital you have at the start of the month. In your first month of operations this will likely be how much money you have in your business account.

2. Projected Income

It's impossible to know exactly how much income you're going to make in any given month. That said, accurate projections can be made based on past sales months, as well as market research.

When calculating income, be sure to account for sales made on credit, which might not necessarily go through in the same month the sale was made. With that in mind, you must also be sure to account for sales made on credit in the previous month that will come through in the current month. Keeping cash and credit sales on separate lines in your cash flow statement can help you to get a clearer picture of where your sales stand.

3. Projected Expenses

This is essentially the reverse of step two. Instead of looking at money going in, you'll be looking at money going out. This includes all regular payments your business makes to stay running including things like the cost of inventory, rent for any properties or equipment, loan payments, taxes, and any other costs you may incur in any given month. These costs should be much easier to account for than your profits as they should be relatively stable from month to month.

4. Total Income and Expenses

Subtracting your total monthly expenses from your total monthly income will let you know if you're profitable or not for that month. The figure you end up with is also the number you'll use as your beginning balance for the next month's cash flow statement.

If you find your total value at the end of the month is in the negatives, then you're going to have to re-evaluate your finances. Knowing what factors bring and take away money from your business, and when they do it, is the key to figuring out how to fix or improve your business. Be sure to take non-obvious factors into consideration, such as how much inventory you carry and equipment you may be leasing.

Simply put, in order to get your cash flow back in the positive you have to either increase the amount of money coming in or decrease the amount of money going out of your business. Ideally, you'll be able to manage both. Increased revenue can come from simply increasing sales. Consider a sale or promotional deal, but remember you'll have to sell more products if you lower your prices. Reduced expenses can come in the form of finding different suppliers or reducing the amount of labour you use. Additionally, a general reduction in the inventory you hold and equipment you use can bring costs down a great deal.

Below is an example of what a cash flow statement might look like.

Cash Flow Analysis							
	January	**February**	**March**	**April**	**May**	**June**	**July**
Beginning Balance	**5,000**	**3,340**	**3,080**	**2,220**	**1,960**	**1,700**	**-740**
Cash Income							
Sales Paid	7,500	7,500	7,500	7,500	7,500	6,000	6,000
Collections of Credit Sales	2,000	2,000	2,000	2,000	2,000	1,600	1,600
Loans & transfers	0	0	0	0	0	0	0
Total Cash In	**9,500**	**9,500**	**9,500**	**9,500**	**9,500**	**7,600**	**7,600**
Cash Expenses							
Inventory	4,500	4,500	4,500	4,500	4,500	4,500	4,500
Rent	1,000	1,000	1,000	1,000	1,000	1,000	1,000
Wages	4,000	4,000	4,000	4,000	4,000	4,000	4,000
Utilities	100	100	100	100	100	100	100
Phone	30	30	30	30	30	30	30
Insurance	1,200	0	0	0	0	0	0
Ads	200	0	0	0	0	280	0
Accounting	130	130	130	130	130	130	130
Miscellaneous	0	0	600	0	0	0	0
Loan payments	0	0	0	0	0	0	0
Taxes							
Total Expenses	**11,160**	**9,760**	**10,360**	**9,760**	**9,760**	**10,040**	**9,760**
Cash at End of Month	**3,340**	**3,080**	**2,220**	**1,960**	**1,700**	**-740**	**-2,900**

SECTION 3: STRATEGY

20. The Customer Journey

The Buyer Persona:

Creating a fictional ideal buyer persona and giving him or her a name may sound silly, but it's really going to help when it comes to marketing. What you can do is draw a picture of a person and write down his or her age and relationship status. Does he or she have kids? What type of lifestyle does your character have? Income? Where does he or she live? What are his or her hobbies?

Write it all down. It's essential to have a clear idea of who your perfect customer is.

Be Flexible:

As you deal with customers you will start to see certain things they have in common. Your product is not for everybody. You can modify, broaden it or narrow it down over time, but you must have a buyer persona in you plan.

WHAT IS YOUR BUYER TRYING TO BUY?

If you have a business selling bottled water, your customer isn't trying to buy water. The chances are, he or she has plenty of tap water at home already. If your customers are middle-class professionals living in the city, your they might be interested in convenience, health and image. Focus on the benefits that your customers are actually interested in buying as opposed to the features of the product. Nobody likes to pay for expensive water, they like to feel healthy with convenient on-the-go products that look good, or they like to avoid disease.

Another example might be if you're selling toasters. Customers might want a budget toaster, or a status toaster or an ultra-safe toaster or an eco-toaster and so on. Once you start to look at this, you can narrow down your marketing and your strategy to reach the right customers with the right type of products.

NEEDS VS WANTS

Understanding the buyer persona will lead you to his or her wants. People buy what they want, not what they need. Once a customer desires your product or service, they'll then try to justify it with logic. Take for example a Mercedes Benz. Does anyone actually need one? Wouldn't a cheaper car be just as useful to anyone needing to get around? Would you be able to find a car that is as reliable and efficient as a Mercedes for less money? The answer is probably yes, but that's irrelevant when you want a Mercedes.

SPEAKING CLEARLY

One of the biggest problems customers have is that they can't understand businesses. When someone has specialist knowledge in an area, they often start to communicate using jargon, expecting the everyone to understand. To your customers it's like you're speaking a different language. When you're trying to communicate with your customers effectively you have to translate your industry speak to something that they can understand. One of the greatest skills a marketer can have is the ability to translate technical language into simple terms.

In some cases, customers might have the technical knowledge to have in-depth conversations about your product or service, but in most cases, even in business-to-business, what you need to focus on is solving problems.

For example: *X does Y*

Don't Talk about yourself all the time

Imagine going to a party and speaking to someone who only talks about him or herself. You'd soon be bored and eyeing up an exit. Don't be the business equivalent of this! Talk to your customers' needs and to their ego, not about how wonderful your business or product is.

Creating a Relationship

Most people don't buy on the first encounter with you. You have to create a relationship.

Don't try to get customers or clients to commit too soon!

If you want to create a relationship with customers or clients, you have to follow the following relationship steps:

1. First, they have to notice you. They might walk past your shop one day and see it, or they may read one of your articles online.
2. Then you have to start a conversation. They might respond to one of your Facebook ads or they interact with one of your posts for example.
3. You continue to interact multiple times without them buying. This could be as simple as them walking past everyday on their way to work and seeing different marketing materials that you have set up. Or it could

be as simple as them consuming your content online several times and seeing your ads.

4. Establish a relationship- Commit to something like signing up to your newsletter. Once your prospects have seen you regularly they will trust you and will be more inclined to making a small commitment like signing up to your email list or to a free trial.
5. Commit to something more like buying a low-ticket product. At this stage, some of your prospects will be ready to make a slightly bigger commitment like purchasing a low cost option that you offer.
6. Purchase bigger item. At this stage some of your prospects will be ready to commit to a higher-value purchase. This could be your full consultancy package or your mid-level or high-level items.

AIDA

The buyer journey is the process that someone goes through before they buy from you. If you have enough social proof through reviews etc.. and you look legitimate, people might purchase from you without you necessarily seeing the journey they've gone through before making that purchase.

In other words, you might not have directly interacted with them as much, but they'll still have done some research on you after noticing you and they'll have had contact with your brand several times.

When you understand this buyer journey, you can plan your marketing around it.

Attention

The first part of the buyer journey is *attention*. This is the first time you notice something.

This is the part of the buyer journey where you apply social media marketing. Social media is all about attention.

Social media marketers often make their content:

Dramatic

Interesting

Sometimes controversial

Eye-catching

Example: Imagine you need a pair of trainers (sneakers) and you notice some nice ones in a shop window or on social media.

INTEREST

Our long-tail content is for the interest phase. This could be blog content, videos, podcasts or resources. It's basically anything that it useful and relevant and that can be indexed by Google. You're aiming to engage the customer's mind here and establish yourself as an expert in your field.

Educating people for free is an excellent way to gain expert status in your customers' minds. It helps them trust you, because you're providing quality and value for free.

A great way to create content like this is to use FAQs. FAQs can help solve common issues your clients encounter. People who approach your business will often come more informed and be easier to sell to, since they've been in touch with your business, you've provided them with value and they have less questions.

Whenever possible, try to create content that doesn't go out of date. This way you're creating long-term assets to recruit customers.

Example: The trainers you've just noticed cost 200 USD but they've been reduced to 100 USD. You have 100 USD to spend. Your mind has already started to intellectualize it and justify the purchase because after all, you can afford these trainers.

Desire

In this stage the customer has made a small commitment like giving you their email. This is intimate and you can now talk to them privately. Within your newsletters there should be an offer where they can take action. You want to create desire. They need to feel that you have a close relationship. It has to be personal.

Example: You try the trainers on and you like the way they look, or you look at pictures online and like the style. You imagine yourself wearing them. Desire kicks in. You want the trainers now.

Action

Here is where you ask for people to decide. You don't need to be spammy, you're asking for a decision on a fair trade. In your newsletter you should offer them exclusive deals and offer them your entry-level products before you market bigger ticket items to them.

Example: On your way out of the shop, a shop assistant asks you if you want the trainers. This is a call to action. You decide that it's something you like and you can afford, so you buy. Online, this could be a pop-up or an email if you have the customer's email address. It could also be done through a retargeting ad on Facebook or Google for example.

21. Creating New Markets: The Blue Ocean Strategy

The idea of a "Blue Ocean Strategy" was first used by Professors Chan Kim and Renée Mauborgne, who introduced the concepts of *red* and *blue oceans* in their international best-seller *Blue Ocean Strategy*.

If you haven't read this book yet, I highly recommend that you do.

The idea is that markets with fierce competition and low profit margins are "red oceans", where it is very difficult to prosper and strategy centres around beating your competition. Some companies break away from these markets and create their own markets where competition becomes irrelevant and strategy centres around creating value through innovation.

You can discover a blue ocean by concentrating on the factors that matter to customers/clients, while ignoring factors they don't care about. In many cases, this attracts a new type of customer that wouldn't have bought from you. The difficult part is identifying an effective strategy and carrying it out successfully.

A lot of mainstream business strategy in the 80s, 90s and 00s was primarily preoccupied with competition. Michael Porter's five forces and the SWOT analysis focus mainly on the environment of the business and its competitors. In these red oceans, market structures are well known and predetermined by the past, as businesses attempt to beat their competitors to acquire customers within the existing market. After time, these markets become saturated and products and services become interchangeable commodities that compete on price. As a result of this ecosystem, profits drop and companies become stagnant.

The situation is made worse by technological breakthroughs in production and delivery, which allow for more efficient supply, outstripping demand and allowing for businesses to keep competing on price.

What you need is a strategy that creates a new market space, a new type of demand, and profitable growth. The market structure has not been established yet in this type of environment.

VALUE INNOVATION

When Renée A. Mauborgne and W. Chan Kim analysed strategic moves over a 120-year period, they found that the pursuit of value innovation was at the core of successful new market creation strategies.

They also found that creating value without any innovation tends to lead to progressive improvements without creating new market spaces or niches. A good example is a business that reduces costs and prices by 3.5%. This is an amazing improvement for the business and for its customers, and it creates a lot of value. However, this won't directly lead to a new market space being created or to the business standing out from its competitors in the long-term.

Similarly, pushing innovation without adding value will often lead a business to focusing too much on new technologies and pioneering, at the expense of customers. It's important to remember that you are here to serve customers and that being a pioneer in the sector must come with a customer focus. A company called Webvan is arguably a good example of this type of mistake. You can find an interesting article on this at techcrunch.com https://techcrunch.com/2013/09/27/why-webvan-failed-and-how-home-delivery-2-0-is-addressing-the-problems/

The ideal balance is arguably to try to do things in an innovative way while still delivering a breakthrough in value to your customers or clients.

New market spaces are constantly being created. The aviation industry, the film industry and the healthcare industry didn't exist in the 1900s. In the 1970s, e-commerce, smart phones, biotechnology and coffee shops weren't industries either.

If you focus on the existing market without any regard for innovation and value, you are not playing to the ever-changing reality of the market. In the next 10-20 years, new sectors will pop up and billions of dollars will be made. There are massive opportunities out there.

According to Renée A. Mauborgne and W. Chan Kim, in the study of 108 new business launches by existing companies, 86% of the launches were incremental extensions of existing markets, but only accounted for 62% of revenues and 39% of profits. On the other hand, only 14% of launches created new market spaces, but they provided 38% of total revenues and 61% of profits.

While this data definitely suggests that creating new market spaces can be extremely profitable, it is easy to forget that they may be riskier, as you are entering unchartered territory

Focusing on creating new market spaces can be very rewarding and profitable, but also very work intensive. With this strategy, you are working to create an untapped marketplace beyond the pre-established market boundaries.

Instead of trying to find ways to squeeze in and compete with established businesses, you are trying to find customers or clients who have been ignored by the sector, or who are currently being underserved. Think of Netflix for example, and how it used the traditional video rental market, combined with the neglected illegal internet download market. It provided a happy medium, whereby, for a small monthly fee, people who used to rent videos and DVDs, could now watch programmes online. It simultaneously attracted illegal downloaders, who were happy to pay for a service in exchange for convenience and safety (fast, accessible, legal and no viruses).

Like Netflix has done, by expanding your efforts in value and innovation, you could potentially reach more consumers or clients and eliminate a large part of the competition at the same time.

Another example of this type of strategy is Starbucks. Starbuck were by no stretch of the imagination the forst coffee shop or even arguably best.

When Starbuck arrived on the scene, there were dozens of coffee shops that were more established. Instead of focusing on the coffee, Starbucks worked to brand itself as an different kind of experience to your run-of-the-mill coffee shop. They reached an untapped level of consumers by offering high-priced coffee, but also by offering teas, smoothies, and Frappuccino. They also offered WIFI and sold CDs and newspapers, encouraging coffee lovers to stay around and chat. This allowed Starbucks to become a social venue and work-place for freelancers the world over.

Questions you can ask yourself to help you identify new opportunities.

- Is the market ready for my product or service?
- Is it ahead of its time or is it the right time to launch it?
- Would it be cost-effective to produce your product or service at the moment, or would it cost too much?
- How much has it cost similar businesses to get up and running? This is vital, as it directly affects the financial forecasts you should start making as part of your business plan.

22. WEBSITE & MARKETING CONTENT

The principles and examples in this chapter are geared towards helping you develop client-friendly writing on your website, promotional materials and even in your business plan. The more human you are, the easier you'll find it to connect with potential customers, clients, partners and investors.

DAWN OF THE 'CORPOBOTS'

We're living in a connection economy where people want to connect with real people. The old business jargon for the sake of business jargon of yesteryear has been demoted to the boardrooms where it's still needed for political games. To connect with humans, you need words that make you sound like a real human, sentences that show who you are, why you're doing what you're doing and why you're different to the 'corpobots'.

When humans switch into the "business" mindset, something dark and strange happens to their brain, they become flesh and bone robots morphing their vocabulary into a meaningless collection of clichés and empty statements - the result is just boring, vague and disjointed communication.

We place greater importance on how someone talks than on the words they are saying alone. Good speaking and writing don't usually do the whole hard-selling approach. They use accessible language as much as possible and focus on adding value, reducing pain or discomfort by solving problems and satisfying a need.

What is your Audience's Pain-Point or Need?

Think about what problems or 'personal hells' your audience is experiencing at the moment. Again, by audience, I mean anybody you interact with for business or professional reasons. It could be a one-to-one negotiation, a sales email or a presentation among many other situations. Think about what personal misery your idea, or product or service saves your audience from. Then, think of all the benefits that they will gain from it and how that will feel. Don't just describe features and benefits of your idea and hope for the best, show them how it feels. Why does your idea matter to them?

GOUSTO UK

This is a perfect example of a company using pain points to show how a product or service solves a 'personal hell'. Think of the 'personal hell' of having to go to do the weekly shop as a single parent of two children with no childcare and no car for example.

Notice how they use the pain-points to empathize with the audience, create rapport and offer the solution. Notice also how they use simple, direct and clear language without any pretense.

This is an excerpt from the "help" section of Gousto's website. https://www.gousto.co.uk/help

'With Gousto you don't need that epic shopping list, soul-crushing queue at the checkout or to take part in the heavyweight grocery bag Olympics. All you need is your weekly box.'

Always Give Details

Giving details is what separates a boring generic text or conversation and a lively, interesting interaction. If possible, try to give extra details and be as specific as you can in your interactions without being anal of course.

For example, say "Pizza Marinara" instead of just "pizza", or say "Northern Pikes" instead of "Fish". You get the idea.

Details are particularly important when you're trying to sell solutions to your audience. It really helps in presentations, testimonials and case studies.

BLU HOMES

This is a great example of a company using details to convey personality and uniqueness. This style lends itself well to presentations, website copy, catalogues and even certain types of emails and meetings.

The following excerpt is from the "Why Blu" section of Blu Home's website. https://www.bluhomes.com/why-blu

The future of home building has arrived.

Unique Innovative Design.

A Blu home is like nothing else. We have been innovatively designing our homes from the ground up for the last 10 years. We design homes to be lived in, with open spaces, lots of windows and floor plans that make sense. You will never look at building a home "the old way" again.

Faster to Build

Our homes are factory built and finished on your site in less than 3 months. Custom homes typically take over 1 year, talk about game changing.

Notice how they give details but keep it simple and clear at the same time. They clearly capitalize on the benefits of Blu Homes over other pre-fab houses on the market.

SIX IMPORTANT POINTS:

1. Stick with short sentences and smaller paragraphs that are easier to read.

2. Within the business plan, try to have bullet points and lists. This makes it easier for a person to read and it will catch their eye a lot more.

3. You should also stick to proper business wording but stay away from useless jargon that doesn't add value, and which can be confusing for someone who is not familiar with the acronym you are using.

4. Do not use small fonts in your business plan, or large ones to make the entire business plan longer. You will want to stick with about 11- or 12-point size and use a typical font like Arial or Verdana.

5. Don't change your font more than twice in the business plan either.

6. You should also be happy with having white space. Don't cram everything together into one long block of text.

Exercise:

Read the following text and change it to make it more personal, direct and interesting. I've provided an example at the end of the exercise so you can check, but there are many ways of rewriting this paragraph. (Please note that this not a real example and any resemblance to any real companies is purely coincidental).

Original text:

"The staff at XYZ Media have been consulting successfully and fostering measureable, tailored solutions for their clients for years. The company's highly experienced media consultants understand and appreciate their clients' requirement to launch and implement cost-effective cutting-edge solutions strategically and systematically. Their sensitivity to the client's objectives, together with their profound expertise in marketing strategy and social media bring added-value and synergy to any project they embark upon."

OK, let's see if we can clean it up a bit...

Write your version here:

....

....

....

....

....

....

....

....

....

....

....

....

Sample Answer

"We've been helping our clients make profit off advertising and social media for years. Our experienced specialists understand and appreciate your need to increase profits and brand recognition by implementing cost-effective solutions logically and systematically. Our sensitivity to your objectives, together with our expertise in marketing strategy and social media will help you achieve your objectives"

Notes:

This sample is by no means perfect. There is still some work that needs to be done, but it's better than the original.

The first thing we've done here is that we've simplified it. We've cut any words that didn't add to the message. Words like *"synergy"* have been cut altogether.

The second thing we've done here is we've reworded some of the business jargon to make it more relatable. There is still some jargon left in this text, but we've tried to reduce it to a minimum. The reader or listener is human, regardless of whether he/she is the cleaner or the CEO of the company. Remember this.

The third thing we've done is, instead of speaking in third person about the company all the time, we've introduced personal pronouns like "we" and personal possessive pronouns like *"our"* and *"your".*

Finally, we've tried to be as specific as possible. We've talked about *"profits"* and *"brand recognition"* rather than "*measureable, tailored solutions*". This not only adds to our overall message, but it also adds credibility and makes us more relatable as a business or business professional.

23. Facebook Ads Masterclass with Jamie Forrest

How to stop overcomplicating your FB ads

When you look at big name marketers like Tony Robbins, Frank Kern whoever else - yes they've got advanced stuff, multiple layers, funnels, upsells, tripwires and all that good stuff...

And yes, it can work great.

But all that is usually very expensive to put together and test and get working.

And for 95% of businesses, it's unnecessary.

I audit a lot of businesses ads accounts, which means I see what is and isn't working, and let me preface my next point by saying the problem normally isn't 'over-complication' so much as it is 'randomness'...

However, I also see a lot of people trying to plan out elaborate funnels (and I've been more guilty of this than most) which are unrealistic, and probably just a form of procrastination anyway.

So to combat that, here are some MVP (Minimum Viable Product) Facebook ads funnels, broken down into different business types.

If you're not sure where to get started, or you've been planning something elaborate for months... stop.

Yes you can add more to these later, but they are bare bones frameworks that work:

LOCAL BUSINESSES (GYMS, HOME CLEANING, RESTAURANTS...)

1. Facebook ad using a Lead Form (Lead Generation objective), with a great value intro offer.

2. On the lead form, ask for a name, email & phone number.

3. Call people up IMMEDIATELY when they fill out the form, and book them in.

4. Keep following up via phone, text, email multiple times for 3 days.

Why it works

• Local businesses have in-built advantages compared to some businesses.

• Being able to call out your audience and location "HEY BOWLING FANS OF SPRINGFIELD" means you can get attention easily, and you already have more trust because you're local.

• An obviously great offer get's people to sign up on impulse.

• By calling people up personally and immediately you keep the momentum going.

• Then you up-sell them after you do a great job on that first offer.

• This isn't about making a profit on the first purchase, it's about getting people in and profiting from the back-end sales.

How to approach it

• Use a genuinely great offer - 20% off something blah blah blah - not good enough, keep coming up with ideas until you've got one that makes you think "shit, I would sign up for this in a heartbeat"

• Follow-up - if you call within 5 minutes of a lead coming through, your chances of getting hold of people are massively increased.

• BUT, also keep calling/emailing/texting back until you get hold of them - these people want what you're offering, but they're busy and easily distracted, so just keep calling and they will thank you for it.

• Solid copy - Here's a simple template to get you started:

[LOCATION/TARGET MARKET]

Do you [WHAT PROBLEM KEEPS THEM UP AT NIGHT]?

Would you like [RESULT]?

Join us as we [TRANSFORMATION OF YOUR PRODUCT/SERVICE] without [COMMON WORRY].

[DETAILS OF YOUR OFFER]

Click now to claim your space before [SCARCITY]

E-COMMERCE/SUBSCRIPTION BOXES

1. Make a 30-60 second video ad of your product, with a link to the product page.

2. Retarget those video viewers with direct response marketing copy (a simple formula like "problem, agitate, solution" is fine). - Link to the product.

Note: When you advertise on Facebook, or have the Facebook pixel installed on a website, then you can create audiences of prior users who have done a specific thing before, i.e watched your video, or visited a specific page on your website. You can then specify that group of people as the audience for a chosen advert. That's what we call retargeting.

3. Retarget those who viewed the product/added to cart with reviews / testimonials / case studies / discounts.

Why it works:

- It uses Facebook's strengths (the algorithm) to your advantage.
- Video views are cheap.
- The more hard-selling ads only go to qualified people.

How to approach it

- For the video ad, use the Video Views Objective, and focus on Showing/Demonstrating your product (intrigue rather than a hard sell approach).
- Test different interests to target initially by splitting them into different ad sets.
- Then create lookalike audiences based on video views/product views/sales as you get them.
- Test continually - this is the basic structure, but you won't know the specific combination of things that work until you test them.
- Be very clear on your numbers (lifetime value of a client, acceptable CPA) and keep them in mind.

SERVICE BUSINESSES (MARKETING, COACHING, ACCOUNTING...)

1. Conversion campaign Facebook ad, which goes to a:

2. Landing page, which offers a freebie in exchange for an email.

3. Send an auto-responder sequence which then sells to them.

Why it works

- Because FB ads are getting more expensive, and email is basically free.
- So if you sell services that require a longer sales cycle, then email allows you to build relationships cheaply and long-term.

How to approach it

- Deliberately DO NOT TRY TO SELL ANYTHING on the FB ad or the free thing.
- Instead, give a MASSIVE amount of value - try to really solve a problem or give a result that your target clients want.

Ideas for the freebie:

- report

- pdf

- video series

- webinar

- cheat sheet

- checklist

- template

- training

• On the thank you page direct them to click a button to download the guide.

• If you've got a FB group, get them to join when they get the download.

Q & A WITH JAMIE FORREST

Q1.

Hi Jamie, I'm a coach and I was wondering, what your experience with a 3 part video series which leads to a conversion page has been.

Answer:

What is the rest of the funnel?

I've had success using video series with coaches - but I'd recommend getting them onto your email list ASAP, because keeping people going through a video series via FB ads has got a lot more expensive recently.

Q. 2

I was thinking...

FB Ad> Landing page with email sing-up> 3 emails with video content solving an issue the individual is facing> conversion page- offering sign-up to my full service.

Or is it better just to use emails instead of video?

Answer:

If the video series naturally leads into the thing you're selling, then that could work.

However, I'd be wary of asking too much of people too soon.

For the first contact, you generally want something they can put into place quickly and get some form of a win.

Who do you coach and what do you teach them?

Q.3

Okay noted- cheers.

I am a career coach, so it's mainly career transition, or how to improve their performance- i.e. "how to get more money or a career they want".

Answer:

OK, got it.

Firstly, I'd say that LinkedIn is obviously a huge platform for you, and you can probably get some good traction on there without paying for ads...

But from the FB ads POV, I would start by putting something together that solves ONE specific problem that people in your audience have - i.e. "3-step template to guarantee the best odds of getting a raise, even if your boss is tight and your numbers are down this quarter"

Then once they're on your list, you could use the video series as part of a launch for your program

Question 4

I'm new to this. Can you explain more what you mean by "Retarget those video viewers with direct response marketing copy (a simple formula like "problem, agitate, solution" is fine). - Link to the product."?

Do you mean you get the viewers' email addresses somehow and then send them marketing emails that link back to your product pages?

Answer:

When you advertise on Facebook, or have the Facebook pixel installed on a website, then you can create audiences of prior users who have done a specific thing before- i.e. watched your video, or visited a specific page on your website.

You can then specify that group of people as the audience for a chosen advert.

That's what we call retargeting.

Question 5:

What would you advise for POD services. Thank you for your time!

Answer:

Print on demand?

The same e-commerce funnel applies, you just need to be really careful with the numbers due to low profit margins.

And then, for the video you'd probably do a slideshow of different products and call out your target market, i.e. HEY GUINEA PIG FANS, YOU'RE GOING TO LOVE THIS RANGE OF HOODIES or something...

Jamie runs his own consultancy called Healthy Leads www.healthyleads.co.uk

Get a Facebook Strategy Audit with Jamie

A Facebook ads Audit is for businesses who are using FB ads to get new clients, but know they could be getting better results.

Jamie and his team can tell you what you're doing well, what you're not doing well, and then give you a clear plan of action for improving things.

If you'd like to contact Jamie for a Facebook Ads audit his email address is jamie@healthyleads.co.uk

24. Use Price Psychology to Increase Profits

Psychological Price-Setting

When you're out buying an item, you probably believe you're basing your decision purely on logic but that couldn't be further from the truth. There are a great number of psychological factors that come into play when making a purchase and according to business-psychology author Gerald Zaltman, 95% of what dictates our purchase decisions, is done subconsciously.

Although this may be troubling to hear as a consumer, it's great news for business owners, as long as you know how to properly take advantage of this fact. We're going to talk about several ways you can more effectively sell your product or service while keeping your prices profitable.

The Decoy Effect

This is about seeking a win-win with your customers so that your most useful product or service becomes your most profitable one as well.

The decoy effect has been known about for some time and it's one of the simplest methods to alter people's impressions of your prices. Essentially, you create useless prices for other similar products in order to push buyers towards what you're actually trying to sell them.

For example, let's say you're currently selling boxes of cookies in two sizes: a small one for $4 and a large one at $9. In this context, most consumers will opt for a small box simply because it costs less. If you want to drive people towards purchasing the large, then you might introduce a third option: a medium box priced at $8.

This might seem counter-intuitive but an investigation by National Geographic, used a similar example and observed that when presented with the three options instead of two, people chose the priciest option more often. The minor price difference made consumers perceive the highest costing item as a bargain. Gregory Ciotti aptly explains this shift in people's thinking.

"The price in the middle, while seemingly 'useless' in there, didn't provide any value but was useful in getting customers to turn from 'bargain hunters' to 'value seekers.'"

"Cognitive bias" is the name for this phenomenon, and it refers to how our minds make decisions based on incorrect or distorted information. Taking advantage of flawed thinking in your own business will require you to know which item you are trying to promote so you can establish decoy prices around it to boost sales. Once again, this technique should be used ethically and responsibly. I am not suggesting for a minute that you set out to manipulate your customers into spending more on crap. The idea behind this technique is that you encourage buyers to seek the highest value and most useful product or service while still increasing your profits. Remember that this is about seeking a win-win not about scamming your customers.

Bundling Items

It's well known that shopping and spending releases dopamine – a chemical known for releasing feelings of pleasure in the body – but it can also cause pain. Carnegie Mellon and Stanford universities engaged in an experiment in 2007 that revealed how prices deemed to be too expensive by consumers actually stimulated the brain region that processes pain. They also saw that lower prices were processed in the region of the brain that handles decision-making.

By selling multiple items under one price tag, you remove the buyer's ability to judge the value of an individual item and you're less likely to cause them pain. Bundles are a common industry practice for everything from software suites (such as Microsoft Office and Adobe Creative Cloud) to cars (features like GPS are bundled into the regular price) and fast food (combo meals).

Bundling is great, but it's possible to lose money if you don't do it right. The key is to not bundle items that reduce the perceived value. Studies have shown that a low-cost item attached to a high-cost one will actually reduce its value in the eyes of the consumer.

Anchoring

Potential customers have a subconscious price in mind that they use when determining if a product is expensive or cheap. Anchoring allows you to influence that reference point and thus improve how your prices are viewed.

A classic example of this method is having an older price listed with a line drawn across it, followed by the new price (ex. $16.95 $12.95). The higher listing is what the customer will use as their reference point, and it makes the lower value look like a bargain.

Conversion expert Jeremy Smith explained what makes anchoring work: "The anchoring effect happens when people make a decision based on the first information that they encounter." It should be noted that there are more ways to anchor than simply striking out old prices.

Anchoring can also be applied to the idea of the product: Apple often focuses on how it feels to use their products, and this distracts consumers from the cost, and even the functionality of their tech.

Another simple form of anchoring is to create a price table, listing your highest costing product or service first which makes that price the buyer's reference point. Think about what number you want your customers to focus on and anchor it by making it the first one they encounter.

FOOT-IN-THE-DOOR TECHNIQUE

Knowledge of this method dates all the way back to 1966 from a study conducted by Scott Fraser and Jonathan Freedman. Their study involved asking one group a small request, followed by a large one a week later (placing a small sticker supporting safe driving on their cars, and then a large sign for the same cause on their properties), while only asking the other group the large request. The study showed that those who had accepted the small request had a higher chance of accepting the large one.

The precise reasoning this works isn't clear, but there are theories. The most probable theory states that people's image of themselves change based on the small favour they completed and thus the odds are higher that they'll acquiesce to requests that align with the values of that previous request.

There's several ways to take advantage of this as a business. A small request can be as simple as asking for a customer's email address. You can entice them into complying by sending them a freebie such as an eBook or a coupon code. One you're able to market directly to the customer, you can send them promotions or offers for exclusive items which they'll be more likely to take you up on as they already agreed to receive emails from you.

Another form of this tactic is the free trial period. Whether it's a streaming service like Netflix, or a subscription software from Adobe, they all offer trial periods to entice prospective customers. When the trial is up, they're more likely to pay for the full service since they're already using it.

Simplify Prices

Prices for a product can get quite intimidating when they're displayed with commas and decimal points intact. Multiple experiments have shown that we perceive prices with more syllables as being higher in cost. So, $2,112.00 seems more expensive than $2112 on a subconscious level. Think about this when listing prices and try to combine it with some of the other pricing practices we've covered. Setting a decoy price with a decimal point (ex. $8.50) could further help drive customers to a product with no decimal point (ex. $12).

25. Find Your Niche

College textbooks have been consistently rising in prices year after year despite vehement protest from students and those in favor of making education more affordable. American senators Dick Durbin, Al Franken and Angus King have gone so far as to propose legislation to counter act these prices which they claim have risen 38% from 2011-2016.

Although lower textbook costs would help students, and marginally increase volume of sales, companies would likely still wind up losing money in such an arrangement. The market for textbooks is actually relatively small. The only people purchasing them are students, who only make up a small total of the population and even then, those students only remain so for anywhere from 2-10 years depending on their program. Textbook sellers already have the market cornered and any increase in sales that might result from a price drop wouldn't even begin to make up for the loss of profit per sale.

Many businesses overextend themselves and lose money by trying to focus on broad appeal. If you focus your own efforts on corner a small market, the same way textbook companies have, you'll find yourself not only in demand, but with more freedom to determine what price you sell your product for.

To start narrowing your market, you need to understand who you're selling to. A generic category like "woman aged 30 to 40" or "teens" simply isn't going to cut it. What kind of work does your target market do? What do they use your product for? How often do the use it? Where do they use it?

Having a firm understanding of your target market can help you maximize your profit in unbelievable ways. Adobe's software programs used to be one-time purchases until they narrowed down who used their product and why. They came to the conclusion that their target market was so dependent on Adobe software that they'd be willing to pay a monthly subscription for the programs in exchange for being consistently updated to the newest version. By switching to a subscription model, Adobe has actually increased their price and profits by catering towards their niche audience and isolating the broader audience.

Starting with a narrow audience doesn't mean that you can't still achieve mass-marketing appeal later down the line. Plenty of products, particularly those in the world, start off by marketing to early adopters and then refining their model to reach a broader audience. Virtual reality headsets are a great example as they used to be a niche product but can now be found at any electronics retailer.

It is possible to start big with a widely appealing product, but this often means you're entering an already established market and competing with big companies who have been occupying that market for a long time. For most businesses, starting narrow is a more sensible strategy.

To find your narrow target market you have to really know who your customer is. It's much easier to sell a product to someone you know than it is to sell to a complete stranger.

You need to connect to your customers and find out what makes them tick. This goes far beyond data gathering online, you need actual input. Survey company SurveyGizmo has published research that states that about 75% of customers are willing to offer feedback to companies if the companies ask for it.

Connecting with customers is important for businesses both large and small. Big names like Elon Musk and Mark Zuckerberg still find time in their days to connect with individual customers through social media and in-person.

Make them feel like they're living in the future. Tesla and Amazon both find success in their progressive use of technology. Amazon sales made up 43% of all online sales in the US. Amazon's Prime member benefits and use of technology like Alexa help to make the online ordering experience easy and intuitive. Ordering items online is as simple as talking to a machine. The ease of use combined with the inherent appeal of the tech involved has made Amazon one of the biggest businesses in the world.

Find your own spin on creating the Amazon experience and you'll naturally draw customers who are willing to pay your ideal price for your product and services.

SECTION 4: GOALS & PRODUCTIVITY

26. The Neuroscience of Positive Habits

THE NEUROSCIENCE OF "PRACTICE MAKES PERFECT"

Everything is made-up of a set of skills you can learn. There is no magic involved. Your brain is flexible like plastic. This means that its structure and connections literally change and adapt as you experience the world around you. This is not some theoretical or mental wooh wooh change, it's actual physical change. Changes in size of regions, shape and structure.

While the biggest changes occur during your childhood and teenage years, it doesn't stop there. For instance, when structural MRI scans of the brains of experienced London taxi drivers were analyzed and compared to the brains of people who didn't drive taxis, researchers found that the posterior hippocampi of the taxi drivers were quite a lot bigger when compared to those of the non-taxi drivers. The posterior hippocampus plays a key role in navigation and mapping. The taxi driver's brains had adapted and actually physically developed to suit their daily routine!

Your brain's continuing plasticity appears to be perfect for lifelong learning, which allows you to adapt to new situations and experiences.

In another study in 2004, a group of adults were studied at the start and at the end of a three-month juggling course. The researchers found that the brain areas associated with the activity had grown considerably by the end of the three-month course. Scientist then asked the participants to rest for three months and scanned their brains after the three-month rest period. Astonishingly, after three months of rest from juggling, the participants' brain regions associated with the juggling had shrunk almost to their original pre-training course size (Draganski et al., 2004).

Use Functional Learning to Boost Performance

Functional learning is essentially practical learning, where you perform tasks to achieve a specified result, rather than just study or memorize information.

1. Functional learning mirrors reality.

In a functional learning exercise, you solve a real problem, typically one that mirrors a challenge you face in real life or work, by using the skills you have to apply every day. This bridges the gap between theory and practice.

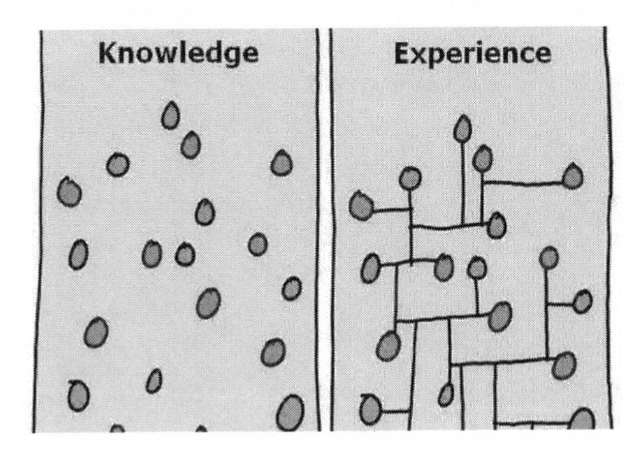

Functional learning produces predictable learning.

Functional learning does not happen by accident. A desired goal may include learning new principles, like the importance of planning, or new practices, like how to be a better presenter. Regardless of the objective, the functional learning exercise revolves around instilling those principles or practices in ourselves.

You never just "wait and see what happens." The learning objectives are designed in advance and incorporated into the process to ensure relevance in the real world. Functional learning exercises are carefully calibrated to produce certain results based on the behaviors and decisions that a you make. Thanks to predictable learning outcomes, you can be confident that you will gradually improve your skills or modify your behaviors.

Case Study: The Habit Loop: How Habits Work

In his excellent book *The Power of Habit: Why We Do What We Do in Life and Business*, Charles Duhigg explains how in the early 1990s, researchers from MIT started suspecting that a section of the brain called the basal ganglia might be key to habit formation. They realized that animals with injuries in the basal ganglia developed issues with routine tasks, such as learning how to run through a maze or remembering how to open a food container. The researchers decided to carry out an experiment that would allow them to examine, at minute scale, the changes and patterns occurring within the brains of rats while they performed dozens of pre-determined routines.

They put the rodents into a simple maze with a chocolate reward at the end. While each rat moved through the maze, the basal ganglia in its brain worked vigorously. When the rats sniffed the air or scratched the wall of the maze, their brain showed lots of activity, analyzing each new smell, texture, image and sound.

The scientists repeated this experiment hundreds of times, watching how each rat's brain reacted as it moved through the same maze repeatedly. A series of changes started to occur. After moving through the same routine hundreds of times, the rodents stopped smelling corners and walking the wrong way. They began to run through the maze faster and faster without stopping.

What was fascinating, however, was that as the rats learned how to move through the maze automatically, their brain activity decreased. As the routine became automatic, each rat went on autopilot and therefore started thinking less and less. The first few times the rats had to navigate the maze, they had to use their full effort to familiarize themselves with the challenge. They had to sniff, touch and scratch. They had to make decisions, make mistakes and then correct those mistakes to find the chocolate.

However, once they had repeated the same task enough, they did not need to scratch or sniff, or even make decisions about which way to go. Their brains had processed the maze so many times that the basal ganglia had mapped the whole process out for them. The parts of the brain associated with decision-making, smelling, and feeling had almost stopped, as they were no longer necessary. The rat's heart rates had also gone down, as they were no longer in an alien environment performing an alien (potentially dangerous) task. They no longer needed to think in order to navigate through the maze perfectly and get the reward at the end.

According to scientists, the results observed during this and many other similar studies, apply to other animals including humans. The brain automatically forms habits in order to save energy and become more efficient and successful at routine tasks needed for survival. Optimizing performance is in our DNA and our brains are constantly working towards this goal.

How to Form Positive Habits

The problem comes when we repeat negative or harmful behaviours or tasks, as the basal ganglia in our brain does not know the difference. The basal ganglia can and will automatically try to form habits if it sees an attractive reward at the end of the maze. For example, if you like the taste of donuts, any habit or process, which gets you donuts, will be an easy habit to form, as the basal ganglia will switch into habit formation mode, regardless of how bad donuts might be for your body. If you hate the taste of vegetables, the basal ganglia will not help you form a habit to get more vegetables into your body.

"This principle is why enjoyment in any form, is so important when it comes to planning your business. Essentially, if you do not like something, you will not do it enough to form effective habits and your basal ganglia will not cooperate either!"

When you are trying to form new, positive habits like projecting your voice, improving your posture or exercising empathy, the trick is not to force yourself to do things you dislike, but to find things within your maze that you do like.

The Zone

"You can either love the process or love the goal."

If loving the goal that you want to achieve were enough, everybody would have six-pack abs and would be president of the world, with Ferraris and unicorns. Loving the goal is not enough, because your brain will not see a real reward at the end of the maze. It will see a long, unpleasant maze that it can easily get out of by just giving up.

"Most processes worth doing are very long, so you need to enjoy the journey"

The only way to achieve anything, from being healthier in the long-term, to getting fit, to achieving success in your career, is to actually enjoy the process of what you are doing more than the result or goal. When you live for the process and you cannot wait to get to work to practice your communication skills, then you will be "in the zone". Once you are in that zone, you will realize that your goals have changed and that your new goal is to be in the process and that the result is a nice side benefit to doing what you want. The world is there for you to take it, so start doing what you want today.

The Power of Dopamine Feedback Loops

Every process of your brain is heavily affected by your emotional state and the same is true for your audience. From what we know about the link between emotions and learning, we know that we learn best under specific conditions, particularly those that result in the release of dopamine. Dopamine is an incredible human motivator and is essentially the reason why gambling can be so addictive for some.

The neurotransmitter dopamine is responsible for delivering sensations of pleasure to the brain as a reward. The chemical is released naturally by the body when we experience success, and it plays a large role in why people become addicted to certain behaviors and substances. You can use dopamine to make your audience feel good and if you use it properly you can even influence them into developing positive habits.

Mark Lukens, Chairman for the Board for Behavioral Health Service North, a major behavioral health services provider in New York, explains that "dopamine is strongly connected to motivation, driving us to repeat the behaviors that create that rush, even when we aren't experiencing it." The actual dopamine rush may be short, but the brain remembers the feeling and how it got there.

The concept of the dopamine loop is what feeds addictions and progress alike. Repeating the same result over and over will still award dopamine, but in smaller quantities each time. In order to get the same rush, or an even larger one you need to up the stakes. For gamblers, this means increasing their wager, for addicts, it means increasing their dosage, and for others, it means seeking a greater challenge.

"Under the right circumstances, this can drive us to seek out ever-greater thrills," Lukens elaborates. This applies to everything from reaching the next level in a video game, to achieving more at work. Let's say it took you two weeks to gain 100 new followers for your business' social media account. You might aim to gain twice as many followers in half the time. Knowing what tasks will not only satisfy you, but your career as well will help you to focus on the important aspects at work.

If you're presenting information or training people, it's important to set up a series of small goals that all work together to create a greater success. Starting out with too large of a goal can actually hurt your ability to have an impact on your audience in the long-run, as failure won't create the dopamine rush which will motivate them to continue. Setting small benchmarks will not only help with focus, it'll keep you and your audience motivated with little hits of dopamine on the way to the big picture objective at the end. As with everything, it's important to balance long term objectives with short term goals.

"Your vision is your destination, and small, manageable goals are the motor that will get you there," explains Dr. Frank Murtha, New York-based counseling psychologist who focuses on investor psychology, behavioral finance and financial risk taking. "Without the vision you're on a road to nowhere. Without the goals, you have a destination but no motor. They work in tandem, and you need both."

We Learn More from Success than Failure

The age-old adage "learn from your mistakes" may need to be thrown away. Studies from The Picower Institute for Learning and Memory at MIT have shown that our learning brain cells are only active in situations where we succeed. Failure does not actually register on a physical level.

Continued success at an activity will help your brain to store the information that enabled that success for longer and thus allow you to learn and improve over time. Each success improves the connection between neurons and releases dopamine, which creates the dopamine loop to encourage your brain to repeat the successful behavior.

The effects of success and failure on the mind were confirmed in a study performed on monkeys where they were made to look at two images on a computer screen. When they looked at the correct image they were rewarded. Monkeys who received a reward for looking at the correct image in one trial were more likely to perform well on the following trial. There was little change in the monkey's who received no reward.

Similar observations have been made in humans, and though we can't make any assumptions, the study suggests that not only does our brain naturally change to adopt successful behaviors, but it barely changes at all when faced with failure.

27. Weekly Business Planner – What´s your ONE BIG THING this week?

About the Weekly Planner

Full disclosure before we start: I shamelessly stole this trick from John Lamerton, who is far smarten than I am. I want to share this trick because, it has had a massive impact on my working life.

FRIDAY: NEXT WEEK'S ONE BIG THING

Every Friday I plan the next week on an A4 sheet of paper. The planner has five columns labelled Monday to Friday and an area at the top to list the things I want to achieve that week.

At the very top, there´s a bright green box which says "THIS WEEK'S ONE BIG THING" in massive capital letters. In this bright green box, I write my most important task for that week. That single most important task has to be something that´s actually going to move my life and my career forward, take me towards my 90-day Goals and push me out of my comfort zone. To check out the 90 Day Goal Challenge go the VIP download section.

I make sure that I always do my one most important task to the detriment of everything else that week

It doesn´t matter if I don´t answer emails for a day, if the result is that I do something amazing that´s going to propel me forward with my big goals. It´s much easier to waste time making coffee, or sorting paperwork or answering non-urgent emails, but when I have little time to spare, I have to make those few hours count. Having your inbox at "0 Unread Messages" is not important, maintaining progress towards your goals IS. If I only do my "one big thing" and nothing else, I´ve already succeeded for the week.

My Daily "One BIG Thing"

THE Power OF ONE

LEADING THE REVOLUTION

As well as the "weekly one big thing", I have a "daily one big thing". I always write my "daily one big thing" on my planner at the top of that day and then draw a big fat line underneath. Then, I write a list of the "small things" I want to do that day. That line is like a barrier in my mind, telling me "you cannot move onto any of the small things until you've done your daily one big thing".

Once I've finished my "daily one big thing", I've succeeded that day, and I can move onto all the other stuff. Even if I don´t feel very energetic one day and I use the rest of the day to answer emails and do small tasks I've still succeeded for that 24 hour period, I've still progressed towards my objectives, I've still got the one important thing done.

HOW CAN YOU MOVE FASTER TOWARDS YOUR GOALS?

Michael

Take for example Michael, a professional swimmer who ate 12,000 calories a day. During intense training phases, Michael swam a minimum of 80,000 meters a week, which is nearly 50 miles. Michael is now retired, but as a professional swimmer, he lived his life by one rule and one rule only. "Will it make me swim faster?" "I fancy a pizza and an evening on the sofa so should I skip training?" "Will doing that make me swim faster?. "No." "Will training make me swim faster?"- "YES, I´m going out to train".

Michael Phelps was the most successful and most decorated Olympian of all time, with a total of 28 medals. Phelps also holds the all-time records for Olympic gold medals and Olympic gold medals in individual events among many other honors. He is a beast of success because he loved swimming and practiced it religiously to the detriment of all the other small stuff. He always put his "one big thing" first. We should all be more like Michael.

No more excuses, you must make doing the "one thing" a habit every day, and over the long-term, you will find that in 6 months you can achieve things that you thought were impossible.

5 Day Planner Challenge

BIG GOAL			
Week Number			
Type of Goal (Business or Personal)			
Day 1			
Day 2			
Day 3			
Day 4			
Day 5			

SECTION 5: MINDSET

28. Stop Complaining

Our Genes Contribute to, but Do Not Define, Who We Are.

We're all spectacularly flawed humans, and we all need to be more proactive in some parts of our lives. This chapter comes from my observations, research and personal experience as a teacher, entrepreneur, coach and human. I've learnt a lot of things about myself and about others in the last few years, as I spend a lot of time one on one with many different people on a daily basis.

Ideas about biologically defined limits can be life-changing. The idea that you are born a certain way, with a certain set of strengths and weaknesses, can have a profound effect on your motivation and on how you feel about yourself. How your brain actually works is that it adapts and changes to be the best it can be in the environment you're normally in. For instance, if you need to navigate routes on a daily basis, your brain will change its shape and the size of some of its areas to become more efficient at navigating.

CASE STUDY: THE TRUTH ABOUT INTELLIGENCE

A 2007 study of teenage students found that students who thought of intelligence as non-fixed and changeable were more likely to gradually increase their grades for the following two years. Interestingly, students who thought of intelligence as a fixed, 'you are what your born with' factor, saw very little change in their grades (Blackwell et al., 2007).

After the initial tests, the researchers then performed an intervention with some of the low-achieving students. They taught the students about how their brain worked and how learning changes the human brain by creating new connections. They drilled into them that THEY were in charge of controlling this process and that they had the power to change their brain through their daily activities. Amazingly, grades for the group of students who learnt about how their brain worked immediately started to improve, while the grades of the students who hadn't received the intervention carried on getting worse!

This highlights just how important it is for you to really understand that YOU are in control of how intelligent and talented you are. Your brain is hard-wired to respond to your actions and your environment, so once again YOU are in control.

If you really want to launch a successful business, it's time to take responsibility for your own learning and your own growth. It's nobody else's responsibility, not your parents', not your partner's, not your boss', not your coach's: it´s you and only you who can succeed. This is your legacy, your blood, your sweat and your tears, no one else´s.

Nobody can make you learn or do anything, unless you like it and want it. You don't necessarily have to like the thing you are doing in that moment, but you have to love the journey that it forms a part of. I personally don't like learning about marketing analytics, but I know it's useful and I love the process of building businesses, writing and coaching. So in a strange way, when I learn about analytics, I enjoy it because it forms part of my journey and it's almost like scratching an itch.

Decisions = Behavior

Behaviour is a manifestation of decisions, not conditions. As Franklin Covey stressed in his bestselling book The 7 Habits of Highly Effective People, "Response-ability" is your ability to choose your response to a situation or an environment.

Too many people do the exact opposite and blame their behaviour on their situation or their conditions. Even worse, they blame their current situation on their past situation. This makes them feel like it's not their fault, but is the equivalent of going into a McDonalds today because you went yesterday, and then complaining that you want pizza. Get a grip. If you look at where you are in life now, it's all a product of your decisions and your choices, your job, your level of income, your relationships, your preparation for exams, 100% your fault, the good and the bad.

People who succeed at an activity do not blame their situation for their lack of success, and they definitely don't blame it on a lack of ability. They try, fail and try again in a slightly different way until they succeed.

People who succeed, take action and actively learn how they can change things that they wish to change. If they want to learn a language they research how best to learn a language and then they go out there and do it EVERY DAY because they love the process of getting better and challenging themselves. If they want to set up a business they research and research and research and try and fail until they succeed.

If you don't already do this, it's definitely not too late, start now.

Love the Process

It comes back to loving the process. If you love what you are doing, then failures and mistakes are not failures or mistakes, they are another step forward in the journey to your inevitable success.

Mistakes and failures should be fun, because they should be learning opportunities and they should teach you more than your successes. If you enjoy what you are doing, then your current situation doesn´t concern you as much, because you are too busy enjoying it.

Understanding the key role of emotion in business separates the best communicators from the rest - not just in terms of results and talents but also in terms of intangible personal assets such as morale, inspiration and dedication. When explaining how great communicators are effective, we describe their strategies, visions, motivation or ideas. However, the reality is that emotions are the crux of great business communication. Leaders understand how to influence emotions and master the art of manipulating them either for good or for evil. It all comes down to how you deal with yourself and your relationships.

29. Your Story is Your Vision

What I'm about to talk about is no secret and is basically common sense, but many people neglect it, or don't fully believe in it enough to implement it. It's based on more than half a century's worth of research into "positive psychology" from institutions including Harvard, Yale and many more.

Imagine for a second we are watching two parallel situations involving two young boys called Jack and Dave. Jack and Dave attend Fleetwood Elementary school in New York, but they don't know each other since it's quite a large school. Jack is feeling anxious and slightly insecure lately. Jack's teachers are generally good teachers, but his Math teacher sometimes mocks him when he makes mistakes. His teacher means well and sees this as harmless, but it makes Jack feel stupid at times. Meanwhile, Dave is feeling happy and secure. Dave's parents are supportive and try to reinforce his social confidence at any chance they get. Dave isn't excelling at school but he's doing OK.

Today is Wednesday and the school canteen is bustling with voices and laughter, as the dinner ladies serve out the kids' food. Jack sits down with his usual group of friends and starts to eat. He is feeling anxious but can't really pinpoint his feelings as he hasn't experienced them before. He realises he forgot to get a knife and fork for his food, so he stands up to leave the table and as he walks away he hears laughter. He suddenly feels more anxious and embarrassed. 'They noticed I forgot my knife and fork and are laughing because I'm stupid' he thinks. Suddenly, a boy bumps into him. 'He did that on purpose', he thinks to himself. The other boy smiles slyly and apologises. 'He must have heard my friends laughing at me'. Jack feels threatened, so he steps back and scowls, then carries on walking.

All the while, Dave has been sitting with his usual friends in his usual spot and realises he forgot a spoon for his chocolate cake. He stands up and walks away. The table where he was sitting erupts in hysterical laughter. He stops and looks back, he thinks to himself 'I missed a really funny joke, I can't wait to get back to find out what it was'. He runs to get his spoon and bumps into Jack by accident. He apologises. He gets his spoon and returns to the table.

These are cycles, and before the children know it, they have formed deep-set unconscious beliefs about how to interpret other people's actions. If Jack continued in this way without breaking the cycle, he may grow up feeling constantly threatened and guarded.

Should adult-Jack blame his teacher for the issues he has? Absolutely not, in my humble opinion. Jack's negative cycle could have started for a number of different reasons. The important thing to focus on isn't what random combination of events started Jack's thinking habits and feelings about the people around him, but the fact that they are not real. They are a completely biased and unreliable interpretation of events based on past-experiences and past feelings which were conditioned to happen. If every time I walked down the street I looked at my phone and walked without watching where I was going, when I smashed my face against the nearest lamp-post I wouldn't accept it as a natural part of walking down the street. Smashing my face into a lamp-post was conditioned to happen because of my behaviour and actions. It would happen again and again until I changed my behaviour. The same thing holds true in these cases.

If as a result of thinking everyone made fun of him behind his back, adult-Jack then chose to be more miserable to his colleagues, this would only cause them to start disliking him and so poor old Jack would have literally created his own reality through his behaviour.

30. THOUGHT PATTERNS

How you tell the story of your past, determines the path for your future

Our brains are naturally hard-wired to criticize every possible move and critically evaluate every situation. It's arguably a survival mechanism there to protect us from life in the wild. The problem is, we don't need it in such an obvious way anymore, so we misunderstand it. The majority of humans don't go out to hunt in packs anymore. We don't chase down giant beasts and kill them with hand-made weapons and we don't have to fend off wild animals on a daily basis. Our brains are an amazing thing, so they have adapted to our new lifestyles. In that adaptation, they have become critical of our every move so as to produce tactical advantages in today's world. The problem comes when we misinterpret that critical view and we become preoccupied with our own feelings. If your brain is telling you that you didn't do something well, it's not intended to knock you down, it's intended as a warning so that you can perfect your technique and gain a tactical advantage.

People who are not overly worried about their own feelings train their brain to see things as they are, no better no worse. Once they are able to do this, they see the situation in their favour and think tactically. This doesn't come naturally to anyone. It comes as a habit that is either instilled in us through our environment and positive thinking cycle (remember Dave) or through practice and hard work. It's one of the most important things you will ever learn to do.

Please note: this doesn't mean you don't see negative situations as they are. It means you realise that depending on how you see these situations, they can help you or damage you. It means that you always find a way to use these 'negative situations' to strengthen you rather than set you back. Whether the glass is half-full or half empty doesn't matter when you trust that you are resourceful enough to find more water.

It's important to understand that every human has insecurities. This is never your fault. However, what you do with the knowledge you have is 100% your choice and your responsibility.

For example:

Reality 1 - Achieving a high score in an aptitude test means you're more intelligent than most people.

Reality 2 - Achieving a high score in an aptitude test means you're more skilled than most people at doing this particular type of test and it only accounts for 25% of job success or income. You have a lot of work to do.

You could argue that both realities are true.

Which type of story sounds more like the ones you tell yourself?

Reality 2 is arguably the most impartial and helpful to anyone who wants to succeed in life.

People with self-awareness and high emotional intelligence often tell the story that benefits them most. If this sounds biased it's because it is, but think about it, if you have to choose between several interpretations of reality, all of which are true, why would you even consider not choosing the most advantageous to you? Why would you ever go out of your way to sabotage yourself and mess your own head up?

How to Identify and Cut Bad Habits

There are two types of things in life: those you cannot influence and those you can influence now. We all worry about a bunch of things every day. As you read this, you might be worried about health, children, problems at work, world peace, or the state of the economy for example.

Many people focus their efforts on the things they are concerned about, which they have no control over yet, which results in accusing attitudes, blaming others, and creating feelings of victimization. They neglect the things they do have control over, so they don´t go forward, and in turn, they feel even worse.

You need to focus all your efforts on the things you have control over now. This is how you grow your knowledge, your confidence and your humanity. Don´t complain, DO.

Be a master of your own improvement. Don´t be a victim of your own bad habits. If you talk to yourself and to others like you are a victim of circumstance, you will never change the things you don´t like or learn the things you want to learn.

So, what do we do with all the failures we've experience in our life? We change those negative memories into positive ones. Using a memory therapy technique that's used to treat PTSD sufferers you can not only remove negative associations from bad memories but actually enhance the positive associations of your good memories.

The method is simple. Take a bad memory, picture it in your mind and slowly allow it to become smaller and dimmer, like the fadeout at the end of a film. Use this dimness to insert new details and rewrite the memory to have a positive spin. You can take a poor presentation you gave and imagine the audience in their underwear, or as a group of monkeys or anything else that might make you smile or make you feel calmer. Keep repeating the memory in your head with these new details and you'll have effectively removed the negative associations.

Apply the opposite method for strengthening positive memories. Bring them to mind and make them bright, loud, and massive in your mind's eye. Keep going over the positive sensations again and again until you feel absolutely unstoppable and let that feeling motivate you.

DO YOU TALK TO YOURSELF?

Be a master of your own life: don´t be a victim of your own bad habits. If you talk to yourself and to others similar to you as if are a victim of circumstance, you will never change the things you don´t like or achieve the things you want to achieve.

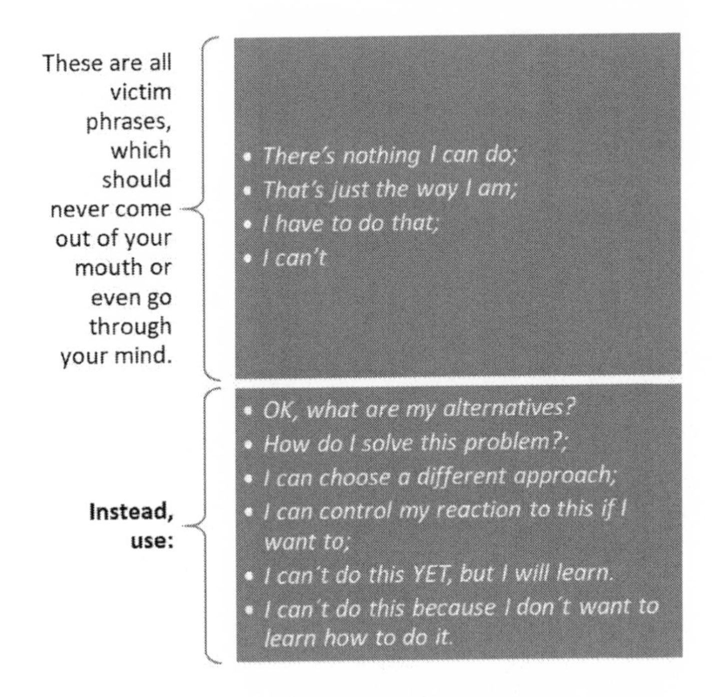

"Whether the glass is half-full or half empty doesn't matter when you trust that you are resourceful enough to find more water."

It's all about the unconscious patterns in your mind. People with high self-awareness focus on the story that benefits them most in order to achieve their goals, while people with low self-awareness tend to focus on the story that creates the most pain or anxiety for them.

This is not to say that you should tell yourself that you're going to be a world-champion bull-shark riding ninja, but refuse to practice your ninja skills or your ability to ride bull-sharks. That would be plain delusional. The idea is to be as impartial as possible in your narrative. For example, instead of saying "I can't do this", you could say "I can't do this yet" or "I can't do this because I haven't practiced enough, but I really like it, and I want to practice, so I will", or "I can't do this because I don't like doing it and I don't want to practice!". Be honest and impartial with yourself, it's only fair.

SECTION 6: MEETINGS, NEGOTIATIONS & PRESENTATIONS

31. Voice & the Importance of Sound

"We often refuse to accept an idea merely because the tone of voice in which it has been expressed is unsympathetic to us." –

Friedrich Nietzsche

The Importance of your Voice

Your voice is key when it comes to communicating effectively in business and in non-business settings alike.

Sound can influence the human brain in different ways and it's a vital part of how we understand the world around us and how we interpret different contexts, whether we're aware of it at the time or not.

Projecting your voice appropriately to fit the situation you find yourself in is central to how people perceive your message. Voice control and projection are key, not only for delivering strong presentations, but for exuding confidence in your everyday life. There are a few basic methods you can apply to achieve this, as well as some vocal exercises you can use.

The Psychological Impact of Voice on your Audience

The easiest way to make sure people are listening to you is to talk in a manner that makes them want to listen. Your tone of voice plays a key role in having people not only listen to what you're saying, but to understand it as well. Tone is comprised of a few key elements: pitch, volume, pace, and emphasis.

People have an instinctive reaction to the tone of someone's voice and you want that reaction to be positive. Think of someone you've heard that has an inviting quality to their voice. A popular example is actor Morgan Freeman. He has a rich, deep, expressive voice that naturally draws attention. His voice alone has given him access to an immense amount of opportunities, including the narration of several documentaries. Contrast that with the voice of someone you don't like to listen to: they're often monotone, nasally, and unappealing overall. Even if what they're saying to you has value, you're less likely to accept their message based on the tone of their voice. We've all had teachers whose voices we just couldn't stand. The right tone of voice can be all it takes to propel you forward.

So, when thinking about your own tone try to emulate the voices of those who successfully capture your attention. This does not mean you should be doing an impression of someone else, but simply working within the natural range of your own voice. You should not have to strain yourself or your vocal cords to achieve a desirable tone.

People who speak in a deeper voice are considered to have more authority than others according to research done by the University of Pittsburgh. Some theorize this connection comes from when physical power was used as a measure of authority and a deep voice generally went hand in hand with a stronger body. So, when you're looking to command the attention of others it's important to use the lower range of your voice, without going so far as to put on a cartoonish voice.

Speaking deeply doesn't mean speaking flatly though. It's important to change your tone as you speak to maintain interest and convey emotional information. Without a variance in tone, it becomes nearly impossible to communicate your excitement, enthusiasm, or even successfully land a joke. If your tone is as flat as a piece of paper then it won't matter how deep your voice is, it's going to put people to sleep.

Perhaps the easiest technique for holding people's attention is to simply speak slower and to emphasize the most important words in each sentence. Not only does it give you more time to think through what you're saying, it gives the listener more time to let your message sink in and truly understand it. It takes effort to actually listen to what someone is saying, so giving your listener more time will help the both of you immensely. Don't be afraid to take a long pause between thoughts as well. A silent moment commands authority much better than attempting to fill the silence with "um" or "uh."

When prepping for your next big presentation, meeting or conversation just remember to talk low, slow, with emphasis and with varied tone.

Vocal Warmups

Right off the bat, it's important to breathe through your diaphragm, and stay relaxed around your head, neck and shoulder areas. You may need to make a conscious effort to do this initially, but you'll notice how, as you form the habit, it will become more automatic.

Our first exercises are going to focus on volume. Increasing the volume of your voice to be louder is an essential aspect of projecting your voice. Be sure you're practicing breathing from your diaphragm. Your abdominal area should expand outwards as you breathe in, and contract as you breathe out to get the best results.

We begin using vowel sounds. Starting with "ah" (as in the word "bar") you will begin vocalizing the sounds softly, and gradually increasing your volume to be loud. Make sure you do this somewhere private or you'll lose all your friends.

It's important to understand that when you're loud, you should not be shouting. Think of the difference between talking to someone directly in front of you, and someone a few feet away. That should be the difference between your soft and loud voice.

Reverse the exercise and go from loud to soft.

If you're feeling a strain on the loud end of things, then you're trying too hard. Remember to be gentle.

Finally, combine the exercises and go from soft to loud to soft to loud, etc. for as long as you like.

This exercise can be done with other vowel sounds such as "oo" (as in "boo"), "oh" (as in "hole"), "aw" (as in "raw"), "ay" (as in "bay") and "ee" (as in "see").

Counting to ten is also an effective volume exercise. You can move gradually, starting soft at 1 and ending loud at 10 or vice versa. You can also make a pattern, having every third number spoken loudly or something similar to that. Play around with it and find what works best for you. Have fun and make it part of your routine.

Voice Projection Exercise

Using a combination of single words, phrases, and sequences you will learn how to project by intoning words and phrases. This means you will emphasize and lengthen vowel sounds, which should create a richer sound. When choosing words and phrases be sure to use words that start with the same sound ("my moaning mother's magnificent mistake"). Watch to make sure you don't tense up the muscles in your head and neck as you perform this exercise. Remember to relax.

Of course, vocal projection can be difficult to master and improper practice of these techniques could damage your vocal cords. If you do not feel confident performing these exercises yourself, or if you begin to feel any discomfort or strain, then stop immediately and find yourself a vocal coach to help you with your technique.

Now that we've seen the importance of sound in communication, let's take a look at some of the barriers our interactions face.

32. POSTURE

"Body language and tone of voice - not words - are our most powerful assessment tools." -

Christopher Voss

BE AWARE OF YOUR POSTURE.

Pop stars, charismatic politicians and actors, are often admired based on the idea that they were born with a special talent for performing. Though there may be some natural talent involved, performance is a set of skills and always has been. This means that you can learn.

As we've seen in other chapters, it's not magic or woo woo energy, it's science. The brain adapts and learns to the environment to which it's subjected. In other words; if you practice, you improve.

Certain habits can make your voice tense, which has a negative impact on your performance as a communicator. If you constantly slouch because you're always looking down at your phone or laptop, this will affect your voice, as you'll be placing extra stress on the neck and voice box area. Try to stand up straight as much as possible and try to monitor and correct your posture as much as possible.

Combine breathing through your diaphragm, and staying relaxed around your head, neck and shoulder areas with a good posture – that means no leaning or slouching regardless of whether you're standing or sitting – and you'll be in a prime position to make vocal projection as easy as possible.

To help keep your posture in check, use an action or event that occurs regularly in your life, such as checking your phone, as a reminder to check in on your posture. Check to see that you're relaxed, your spine is straight, and you're not accidentally clenching your teeth or unnecessarily straining parts of your body.

It's important to remember that projecting your voice should not be causing any strain on your cords or any other part of your body. If you feel any strain, then you're not projecting, you're yelling. Remember to focus on being gentle with your vocal cords as you practice and to reassess your technique if you start to feel any strain.

33. Barriers to Effective Business Communication

“The most important thing in communication is hearing what isn't said.” –

Peter Drucker

WHAT'S IN IT FOR THEM?

The world is full of constant distraction in the form of media, entertainment, social interaction and many, many other things. People automatically grab for their phones whenever they have a spare few seconds. Even billboards are becoming less and less relevant as a marketing tool since most people's attention while they sit in cars is now down towards their phones.

Why should they listen to you? Why should anybody listen to anyone else?. *"What's in it for me?"* - This is what we all instinctively ask ourselves when we start reading something or listening to someone.

It's not just about what you have to say, it's about how you deliver your message and about whether your message is valuable to your audience. You need to be helping your audience in some way for them to stick with you. This is what you should be focused on when you speak, write and present.

In a world where attention is so fickle, if you want people to listen to you, you need to grab them and keep them long enough for them to hear your message. There is constant temptation to become distracted, so you need to get good at the attention game.

If one were to seek out an unconventional definition of communication, it would be, Brain to Brain marketing, since communication is the meeting of minds. Communication is devoid of words, sentences, paragraphs and the entire spectrum of linguistic tools and methods. In its truest form, it is two nervous systems exchanging information. It is effective when the circumstances are as unbounded as possible.

Barrier 1: Using Meaningless Language.

We're all guilty of this now and again, but it really is a communication killer because it sucks the power and meaning out of whatever it is you're saying.

Sometimes we resort to hyperboles, like “incredible” and "awesome" to talk about relatively uninteresting things, such as when someone has bought a new hat. We often do this to please others or make them feel at ease, but while it may be intended as a gesture of goodwill towards the other person, it can come off as insincere and can shape other people's perception of what we consider to be "incredible". If everything is "incredible" then nothing we describe will ever truly be incredible.

Barrier 2: Ego

Another thought pattern that damages the effectiveness of our communication is our fear of being seen to be wrong. When we're overly concerned by this, it can distort our interpretation of the messages we get from other people and from our environment. This will in turn, influence our response.

Barrier 3: People Pleasing and Seeking Approval

People pleasing, or seeking approval from others is another surefire way to damage and distort your communication at work.

Although peer pressure is probably more obvious among teens, it definitely carries on into adulthood in more subtle and unconscious ways. We buy certain things to keep up with the Jones' and we all say certain things to be seen in a certain light to some extent, whether we admit it to ourselves or not. If we let this behavior get out of hand, we become people pleasers and others see straight through this. People pleasers often come across as insincere and manipulative. People will not respect our message if they do not respect our values.

34. THE NEUROSCIENCE OF WORLD-CLASS PRESENTATIONS

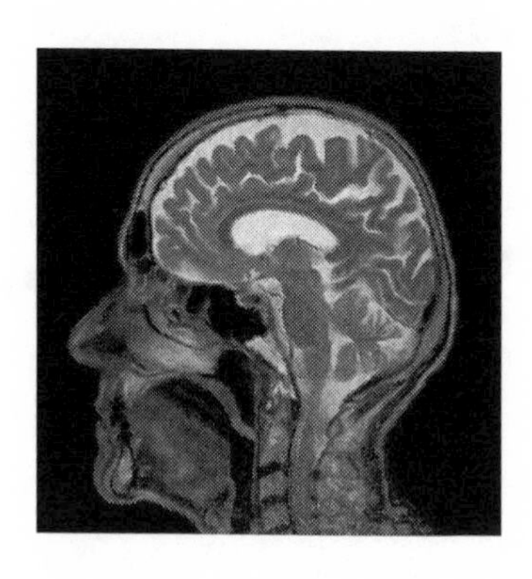

THE MULTI-MODAL TECHNIQUE

Engaging with material in multiple formats, such as combining text with a visual representation, can improve your audience's memory of the concepts or ideas being presented (Paivio and Csapo, 1973). Hardly rocket science is it, but so many of us throw common sense straight out of the window the minute we sit down to plan a presentation.

This is what the idea of multimodal education is based on. Multimodal education emphasizes combining learning methods in order to better teach students. This technique has been proven to increase brain activity beyond the point of what using a singular method can produce (Beauchamp et al., 2004).

More important than an increase in brain activity is where that activity takes place. Studies saw increased activity in the superior temporal sulcus and middle temporal gyrus, which are both responsible for multisensory processing. The fact that this region of the brain switches on automatically when exposed to multiple stimuli suggests that it plays a large part in the improved memory that results from multisensory exposure.

So say you have a presentation coming up, try to combine images or even short videos (if appropriate), with small amounts of clearly expressed text and speaking. Keep shifting between the different 'modes' to keep your audience's brains as active as possible.

The positive effects of combining mediums on memory can be seen in a study in which participants had their brains scanned as they were given a memory test where they had to memorize pairs of objects. After the test, participants filled out a questionnaire about what memorization techniques they used to help them complete the task. Though self-reporting can be an unreliable method of gathering information, the brain imaging showed that people who combined auditory information with the images they saw, techniques as simple as saying the names of the objects they saw aloud, performed better than those who didn't. The study concluded that engaging with material in multiple different ways made a stronger impact on the people's memories (Kirchhoff and Buckner, 2006).

Using Stress to Enhance Memory

Another factor that can have a positive effect on your audience's memory recall when you present your business plan is physical and psychological stress. Interestingly, stress must be occurring at the same time as the event that you wish people to recall or learn for the memory enhancement to happen (Joels et al., 2006). Stress that occurs before or after the event has been shown to actually be detrimental to memory (de Quervain et al., 2000; Kirschbaum, 1996; Kuhlmann, 2005).

This doesn't mean that you should make your presentations ultra-stressful by shouting at people or by setting off the sprinklers on them, but it does mean that you can benefit from adding a small element of stress through practical demonstrations or activities for instance. During your product demonstration, you could add something as simple as a time limit to inject low levels of stress and excitement.

'Chunking' Information

Our working memory serves as a temporary store for new information we are processing. The average limitation on a working memory is roughly seven individual pieces of information, though this number can vary based on the individual and their educational achievements (Pickering, 2006). Our working memory is what we use for everything from writing down a phone number (which is why we often like to get the info in small pieces rather than all at once) to learning a new skill or concept.

Try to use this knowledge if you need to present your business or product so you don't overload and ultimately lose your audience. Deliver the information to your audience in small digestible chunks so that they can process it.

It's also worth noting that external representation of information (such as the written down phone number or a written-out math equation) can help take pressure off of the working memory and increase efficiency. This is similar to when you close down unnecessary programs on your computer to free up the CPU and the system. As result of this, the computer speeds up and can process tasks faster.

35. EMPATHIZING WITH YOUR AUDIENCE

"There is a difference between listening and waiting for your turn to speak."-

Simon Sinek

EMPATHY

Psychologist Edward Thorndike spoke of "social intelligence" as the ability to understand people and social relationships. Just as attempts have been made to measure intellectual ability in the form of Intelligence Quotient or IQ tests, so have we attempted to understand emotional intelligence with EQ tests. Empathy is one of the main qualities found in emotionally intelligent people. Empathy is not exactly the same as sympathy although the two are very similar.

Think of empathy as "Advanced Sympathy"

Sympathy means recognizing someone's pain and responding accordingly and consciously with some form of support, for example with hugs or reassurance. But the person feeling sympathetic is still somewhat of an outsider to the actual emotions being experienced and felt. Empathic people literally feel the similar emotions to the people they are around. For example, they don't just feel sorry for someone - they feel that person's sorrow as their own. Parents usually have a somewhat empathic connection to their children.

Research on empathy shows that just as psychopathic behavior has neurobiological roots, there is a part of the brain called the right Supramarginal Gyrus, which recognizes instances where there is no empathy and corrects this behavior. What is interesting is that in instances where quick decisions need to be made, this area of the brain doesn't function as well as it usually does, reducing our ability to empathize. This is an actual observable phenomenon as scientists are able to see which areas of the brain light up more during certain situations through scans. When certain parts of a patient's brain are damaged, we've been able to see the results in the changed behavioral patterns of that person. Some brain lesions can disrupt a patient's ability to interpret body language or to share and understand other people's emotions, creating an inability to empathize. (Hillis, & E., A. 2013).

THE TRUTH ABOUT EMPATHY

Most of us are guilty of speaking more than we listen, as we like the sound of our voice at times. True empathetic listening, is listening with the intention of understanding. It's essential that you do this with your customers and investors if you're seeking investment.

Empathetic listening is powerful in business, NOT because "it's what nice people do", or because "it's the right thing to do". Those things are true, but empathetic listening is powerful because it provides you with accurate data on the person or group you are aiming to reach.

In order to truly help another person and make a difference in their life, you need accurate data. Obviously, getting to know other people and learning about their stories is very interesting in itself. However, the practical value lies in the data they are giving you about themselves. How can you achieve a win/win unless you have the data? The answer is, in my experience, you can't.

THE BASIC DYNAMICS OF NEGOTIATIONS

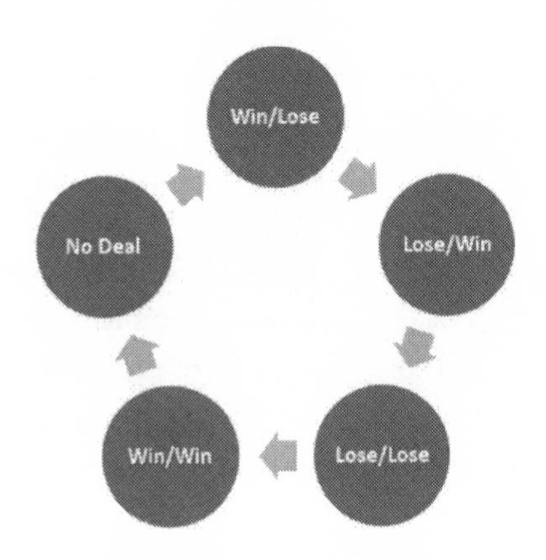

In his bestselling book *The 7 Habits of Highly Effective People: Powerful Lessons in Personal Change*, Stephen R. Covey presents these five possible results of human interaction. They represent the mentality and possible general outcomes of any interaction between human beings. The sixth paradigm "Win", is missing, because a "Win" mentality, when someone doesn´t care about the outcome as long they win, inevitably leads to one of the other paradigms. ⍰

Win/Win. — is a way of thinking, which tries to bring value to other people without accepting injustice. Interactions with other people are not battles but collaborations for mutual benefit and value.

Win/Lose. — This is an attitude that tries to establish a situation where you win and the other side loses. While this is necessary in competition and war, it is arguably only beneficial in these particular situations, and not in everyday interactions (business or personal). For example, win-win with employees, colleagues, partners and customers is far more effective and beneficial long term. Win-lose might be appropriate with competitors for example.

Lose/Win. — This is what gave "nice guys" a bad reputation. The problem is, real nice guys don´t play this game. This game is more for "scared guys". When someone allows people to do things in order to avoid confrontation, it can cause a lot of damage to everyone involved.

Lose/Lose. — This is when two win-lose people, departments or businesses get together. Nobody wins here.

No Deal. — the interaction may lead to no agreement or no production of value to any side. This is a No Deal.

What are Win-Win people like?

They have integrity — they value themselves as a person of consistency and have a specific moral code, which they follow.

They are mature — they have an understanding of the world, from a "big picture" standpoint

They have an abundance mentality — there is plenty out there for everyone. We can all benefit from this opportunity!

EMPATHETIC LISTENING TIPS:

Empathetic listening creates stronger relationships with clients and customers.

1. Put the feelings and thoughts of your clients or customers before your own as long as it's fair. Remember that contrary to the saying, the customer or the investor isn't always right. Exercise common sense and don't let anybody walk all over you. If you feel strongly about something, follow your gut.

2. Let your guard down and be open with your emotions and opinions if possible.

3. Imagine yourself in the experiences and perspectives of your customers, clients or investors.

4. Avoid judgment or criticism when you get feedback. Decide if the feedback you're getting is fair, and if it is, act on it! Don't get upset or take it personally.

If you apply these principles you'll understand your customers better and, as a result, build closer more meaningful relationships. The more you apply these principles the more people will want to share with you, try it and see.

36. YOUR WORDS MATTER

"As we express our gratitude, we must never forget that the highest appreciation is not to utter words, but to live by them." -

John F. Kennedy

Think About Your Words

When focusing on improving our presentation skills we often look at some of the best presentations in order to mimic the techniques of icons like Steve Jobs, or VaynerX's Gary Vaynerchuk, but it can be just as valuable to look at bad presentations to see what kind of mistakes we should avoid.

We'll take a look at a couple arguably dreadful speeches and presentations to see what went wrong, and what can be done to avoid these scenarios ourselves. These speeches are listed in Vanessa Ong's excellent 2017 article *15 Bad Speeches We Can Learn From*. I urge you to check it out when you have a minute ☺

MINI-CASE STUDY: MISS TEEN SOUTH CAROLINA 2007

Take an infamous speech made during the Miss Teen South Carolina show in 2007.

A part of the Miss Teen competition demands that participants answer a "thought-provoking question" in order to demonstrate their higher thinking abilities. The questions are selected at random and Miss South Carolina was asked the following: "Recent polls have shown that one fifth of Americans can't locate the US on a world map, why do you think this is?"

She begins by slowly explaining that some "US Americans" don't have maps and she ends with a vague suggestions that the United States education system should somehow benefit South Africa and Iraq. This is what happens when you charge headlong into a question you are completely unprepared for.

Before we scoff at Miss Teen Carolina, let's get off our high-horse and be honest with ourselves, I'm sure most of us can recall a situation when we've jumped head-first into answering a question and then realized half-way through that we're talking absolute nonsense. It can be a horrible, embarrassing feeling when this happens. So, what can we learn from this?

Lesson 1: Be prepared.

Managing a presentation of your business or product as an entrepreneur requires you to be aware of two things: the message you want to deliver to your audience, and the information your audience might want from you. During election campaigns, politicians have to be able to speak on a variety of different issues, from education to environmental policy and more. If you make sure you know your business inside out, then you'll drastically decrease your odds of being caught out during the big moment.

Lesson 2: Take your time when answering a question.

You are under no obligation to answer questions as quickly as possible; it's a presentation or a meeting, not a race. Do not be afraid to ask someone to repeat their question or to pause and consider the question before answering. If you truly don't have an answer for someone, be honest with them and tell them you will get back to them after you find the answer. Not only will you avoid embarrassment in front of an audience, but you'll come off as thoughtful and honest. People respect honesty and "cojones", so show them you have both!

37. Eye Contact

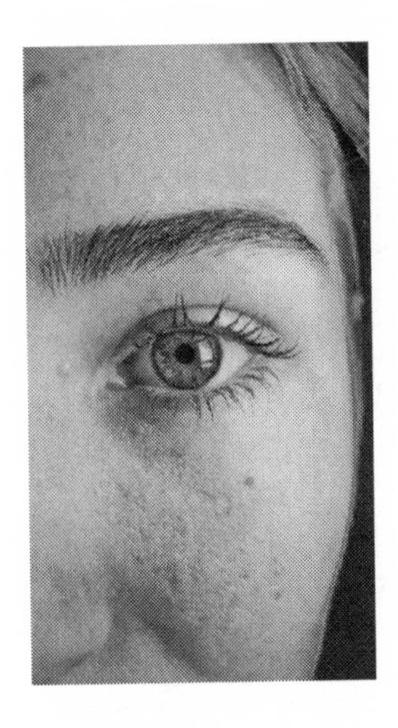

The importance of eye contact in Western cultures is undeniable. Neglect eye contact and your audience will assume you lack confidence at best and that you are untrustworthy at worst.

It's easy to mess up and really hard to do properly. If you do it too much it becomes threatening; but then, not enough of it can have the same effect. This is the exact reason why one-on-one interactions often go hand-in-hand with private brain meltdowns *"Do I make eye contact again now? Is it too much? How long is acceptable before looking away?"*

In a study done by Japanese researchers, volunteers watched a video of someone's face whilst solving a word challenge in which they had to think of verbs to match different nouns. For example if they heard "ball" the word "kick" would be logical.

Amazingly, as soon as the face in the video appeared to be making eye contact with them, the volunteers started having problems with the more difficult nouns. Even with a stranger in a video, eye contact is so powerful that it uses the person's cognitive reserves, leaving him or her unable to effectively concentrate on anything else!

Practice gazing towards your audiences' face or faces to strengthen the connection while you're delivering your message, but don't worry too much about making actual eye contact all the time. A recent study using eye-tracking technology carried out by ECU researchers gave surprising results as to the importance of eye contact.

During the study, one of the researchers engaged short four-minute conversations with 46 test subjects. In the conversations, both people wore eye-tracking goggles. For around 50% of the interactions the person conducting the tests looked at the subject's eyes the majority of the time, and for the other 50% he gazed mostly at the mouth.

Following each of the conversations, the volunteers evaluated how much they enjoyed the interactions. In the conversations where the researcher had been looking mainly at the volunteers' mouths, they reported the same levels of eye contact and enjoyed the interactions just as much as when the researcher made direct eye contact.

This research suggests that gazing at people's face produces the same effects as direct eye contact. So if you're not 100% comfortable with making confident eye contact all the time don't get too hung up on it. There's no need to try to make eye contact with your audience, instead just gaze at their faces.

38. Don't Be Foolish

"Any fool can make something complicated. It takes a genius to make it simple."

Woody Guthrie

COMMUNICATING CLEARLY

The techniques looked at so far won't do much good unless your message is clear and concise. Language is a powerful force and it can be used to help or to confuse and damage. The problem comes when we wrongly confuse the language used to confuse and damage with good communication.

In this section, you'll learn the principles of clear, powerful business communication. In the process of doing this, you'll not only improve your speaking and writing skills; you'll hopefully see the beauty and importance of clarity.

Can you think of anything more mind-numbingly frustrating than struggling through a business contract, trying to make sense of the unnecessarily dull legal speak while dealing with crucial things you need to know?. Or desperately attempting to remain focused while you're reading a pompous academic paper on what would have been a gripping topic, had the researcher written it thinking about the reader?

39. Clear Communication Checklist:

1. Keep your sentences simple and direct
2. Remove unnecessary business jargon to make your communication more effective and powerful. Remember that no matter who you're writing or speaking to, they are human, so relate to them as a human.
3. Avoid the third person if possible. Speak about "us" and "you" if possible.
4. Be as specific as possible. Don't ramble on about "*measureable, tailored solutions*" when your audience is interested in *"profits"* and *"brand recognition"*
5. Avoid the Passive Voice like the plague, unless you have no choice. Instead of saying *"the project was launched by Gary"* use an active sentence like *"Gary launched the project".* Active sentences tend to sound more alive and as a result more interesting.

BONUS: FREE BOOK! THE PRODUCTIVITY CHEAT SHEET

Download your free copy of The Productivity Cheat Sheet: 15 Secrets of Productivity here!

https://www.idmadrid.es/vip-resources

IDM Business & Law Academy

EXTREME
PRODUCTIVITY
PLANNER
The 30 Day "No Excuses Productivity Planner". Includes
15 Secrets Successful People Know About Time
Management. (Extreme Productivity Planner Series)
MARC ROCHE

About The Author

Learn more about Marc at
https://www.amazon.com/Marc-Roche/e/B07FZ9S1V6?ref=sr_ntt_srch_lnk_1&qid=1548070478&sr=8-1

Learn more about Marc's Publishing & Media Company at
https://www.idmadrid.es/vip-resources

OTHER BOOKS BY MARC ROCHE

Business English Writing: Advanced Masterclass- How to Communicate Effectively & Communicate with Confidence: How to Write Emails, Business Letters & Business Reports. Includes 100+ Business Letters

Master Legal Vocabulary & Terminology- Legal Vocabulary In Use: Contracts, Prepositions, Phrasal Verbs + 425 Expert Legal Documents & Templates

IELTS Writing Tasks 1 & 2 Advanced Masterclass: Band Scores 7.0 - 8.5: IELTS Academic Writing Book 1

THANK YOU

If you enjoyed this business plan book or found it useful, I'd be very grateful if you'd post a short review on Amazon.

Your support really does make a difference and means a lot to me. I read all the reviews personally so I can get your feedback and make this book even better in the future.

Thanks again for your support!